Presented To

_____

Presented By

_____

On This Day

The LORD has done great things for us,
and we are filled with joy.

PSALM 126:3

Promises of Joy: A Daily Devotional

Copyright © 2005 by The Zondervan Corporation

ISBN-10: 0-310-80717-4

ISBN-18: 978-0-310-80717-9

Requests for information should be addressed to:
Inspirio, The gift group of Zondervan
Grand Rapids, Michigan 49530
http://www.inspiriogifts.com

Compilation: Rebecca Currington in association with Snapdragon Editorial Group, Inc.
Project Manager: Tom Dean
Design Manager: Val Buick
Production Management: Matt Nolan
Design: studiogearbox.com

Printed in China
05 06 07/CTC/ 4 3 2 1

PROMISES
OF JOY
A DAILY DEVOTIONAL

inspirio™

INTRODUCTION

The Bible says that a merry heart is good for your health. That's why we've created *Promises of Joy*. It's our hope that as you read, you will receive a dose of joy each day, leaving you strong and healthy in every way—physically, emotionally, mentally, and spiritually.

So begin right away and expect God to meet you each morning with a joyful word to help you deal with all the issues that impact your life. He's waiting—ready to bless you with wisdom, understanding, insight, discernment, and joyful thinking.

THE PUBLISHERS

Joy is the most infallible sign of the presence of God.

LEON BLOY

MONDAY

ONE TRUE HAPPINESS

You will call upon me and come and pray to me,
and I will listen to you.

JEREMIAH 29:12

C hristians often complain that private prayer is not what it should be. They feel weak and sinful. Their hearts are cold and dark. It is as if they have so little to pray, and in that little, no faith or joy. They are discouraged and kept from prayer by the thought that they cannot come to the Father as they ought or as they wish. Child of God, listen to your teacher, Jesus! He tells you that when you go to private prayer, your first thought must be this: The Father is in secret, and the Father waits for me there.

Do not think about how little you have to bring to God. Instead, think of how much God wants to give to you. Just place yourself before God and look up into God's face. Think of God's wonderful, tender, compassionate love. Just shut the door and pray to your Father who is in that secret place. Isn't it wonderful? You are able to be alone with the infinite God and to look up and say, "My Father!"[1]

ANDREW MURRAY

TUESDAY

❋

NEVER TOO LATE

There is a time for everything,
and a season for every activity under heaven.

ECCLESIASTES 3:1

My little Irish grandmother, at the age of 100, participated in a family reunion with her ten children, their spouses, and their children. The reunion was held on the old family farm where the ten "kids" had been raised. As they were organizing a baseball game to be played in the back field, my grandmother insisted on playing. When she hit a fly ball high into left field, her eldest son offered to run bases for her. "Are you kidding, Basil?" she snorted. "You're eighty years old," and off she trotted. She lived to be 103.

God has created within all human beings a tremendous drive to survive and a capability to succeed to the level of our God-given gifts. Isn't it fantastic to realize that most of us have barely tapped into our potential? We could be creating and contributing so much more. Are you living out your potential?[2] Doing so will fill your journey with joy.

MARILYN MEBERG

WEDNESDAY

✦

ORDINARY MOMENTS

You will fill me with joy when I am with you.
You will give me endless pleasures at your right hand.

PSALM 16:11 NIRV

It is often in the small things that I recognize God's presence and can sense his kindness and tenderness.

My friend Allyson's baby, Logan, seems to have an inner joy that comes straight from heaven. One day as Allyson and I were running errands, she left me in the car with him. Every time I turned to look at him he would giggle with such zeal that I wondered whether he could catch his breath. Any sadness I felt that day was washed away as I listened to Logan laugh.

Once, hurrying through an airport, I came upon a lady in a wheelchair. Amidst the people rushing around us, my eyes met hers. The sweetest smile appeared on her face. I smiled back, but I knew she would never fully realize how that small gesture had filled my soul.

I believe that God is in our every day. Many moments occur in our lives that reveal his face, his touch, his voice. Look for him today. He will be found.[3]

KATHY TROCCOLI

THURSDAY

✦

SIMPLE TRUST

Blessed are those who trust in the LORD,
whose trust is the LORD.

In God's infinite plan, he allowed me to be born out of wedlock to a crippled girl whose parents were so embarrassed that they forced her to leave home. My great-grandmother convinced my mother to let me live at Granny's house. Granny and my great-grandfather, Daddy Harrell, became very attached to me. Daddy Harrell and I became best friends. He was blind, but as soon as I was old enough, I became his eyes and led him down the street to the doctor's office, to visit his friends, or to church.

Just as Daddy Harrell trusted me to lead him without fear, he taught me to trust God by turning over to him my fears and anxieties. God knew my great-grandparents' nurturing would be the catalyst that would propel me to learn the truths about who God is and how he works in our everyday lives. I know my heavenly Father because I have seen him in the people I love.[4] It has filled my heart with joy.

THELMA WELLS

8 PROMISES OF JOY

FRIDAY

A HEART REFINED

Consider it pure joy…
whenever you face trials of many kinds.

JAMES 1:2

I love you, God," we say, but we deceive ourselves unless that love is proved. Love will say, "I'd do anything for you, God, follow you anywhere." Obedience will say, "…and let me prove it." Obedience is not so much for God's sake, but for ours. God wants us to realize the depth of our love for him.

He is the one who brings us into prisons and lays burdens on our backs. All the while he never withholds his love from us. His love drives him to test us in order to refine us like silver. When gold is put through a refining process, it involves heat. But when silver is refined, it involves pressure. When a test heats up, we want to escape; when a trial is pressuring, we want to collapse. If we remain faithful and rigorously obey, our hearts become refined. Obedience melts away pride and prejudice. Obedience crushes into dust self-centeredness, revealing a heart pure and at peace.[5] A heart of pure joy.

JONI EARECKSON TADA

WEEKEND

❖

UNEXPECTED DELIGHTS

The LORD heals the brokenhearted
and binds up their wounds.

PSALM 147:3

Each of us has something broken in our lives—a broken promise, a broken dream, a broken marriage, a broken heart…and we must decide how we're going to deal with our brokenness. We can wallow in self-pity or regret, accomplishing nothing and having no fun or joy in our circumstances, or we can determine with our will to take a few risks, get out of our comfort zone, and see what God will do to bring unexpected delight in our time of need.

Ernest Hemingway puts it this way in *A Farewell to Arms*: "The world breaks everyone and many are strong at the broken places." I challenge you to be one of the many. Take that step of faith and ask God to surprise you in a unique way that only he has the flair to accomplish.[6] You'll find it most delightful.

LUCI SWINDOLL

Heavenly Father, I give you the broken places in
my life and ask you to make me strong in these places.
I trust you to take me beyond my comfort zone,
so that I can experience fullness of joy. Amen.

MONDAY

SUPERMOM

Praise be to the Lord, to God our Savior,
who daily bears our burdens.

PSALM 68:19

We all want to be a good example for our kids—but how often do we consider what that really entails? In addition to changing diapers, running carpools, and helping with science projects, godly women are supposed to be wise, resourceful, hospitable, encouraging, diligent, creative, generous, faithful, watchful, vigorous, strong, and cheerful—and that's just for starters! If you think I'm making this up, take a look at Proverbs 31.

This passage used to discourage me. But that's where Jesus comes in. There will be times when I let my children down. But I have learned that the less I rely on my own abilities and the more I rely on Christ—and the more I let my children see me depending on him for wisdom, guidance, and strength—the more I will be able to set an example that's worth following. Instead of saying, "Look at me," I'll be able to say, "Look at Jesus."[7] It takes the burden off of me, so I can experience his joy.

JODIE BERNDT

TUESDAY

✦

GOD IS NOT DEAF

Those who suffer he delivers in their suffering.

JOB 36:15

No one has expressed pain and unfairness better than Job. Yet behind those words of anguish lies a darkly shining truth: Job—and you and I—can, through obedience, join the struggle to reverse that suffering. Job paints the drama of faith in its starkest form: the best man on earth suffering the worst, with no sign of encouragement or comfort from God. The fact that Job continued to trust him, against all odds, mattered. In God's speech, clearly the wonder of creation that impressed him most was Job.

People who suffer still find themselves borrowing Job's words as they cry out against God's apparent lack of concern. The book of Job affirms that God is not deaf to our cries and is in control of this world, no matter how it appears. His very presence caused Job's doubts to melt away. Job learned that God cared about him intimately, and that God rules the world.[8]

God promises to deliver those who suffer; and just as it was true for Job, you, too, will experience joy again.

PHILIP YANCEY

WEDNESDAY

❖

A FESTIVAL TO BE ENJOYED

*They will celebrate your abundant goodness
and joyfully sing of your righteousness.*

PSALM 145:7

One of the best statements about joy I've ever heard was made by Luci Swindoll: "Life is a happy thing, a festival to be enjoyed rather than a drudgery to be endured."

Who wouldn't jump at the chance to experience life as "a happy thing" rather than as a never-ending "to-do" list? But sometimes enjoying life is easier said than done. When the phone is ringing, the kids are tracking mud across the carpet, your coworker isn't pulling her weight, your best friend is snippy, and your husband responds to your furrowed brow with his ever-sensitive "What's wrong with *you?*" finding the joy in the situation doesn't come naturally for most of us.

If we're to get beyond the drudging and trudging to celebrating the abundance God promises to those who know him, then we need his perspective. We must uncover the beliefs and attitudes that keep us from experiencing the abiding joy we can have even in the mundane or frustrating moments of life.[9] Ask God to reveal them today.

TRACI MULLINS

THURSDAY

❋

INFECTING OTHERS WITH JOY

A cheerful look brings joy to the heart,
and good news gives health to the bones.

PROVERBS 15:30

There are days when I start feeling blue. On those days
I've learned to avoid certain things. I won't weigh
myself, listen to sad music, get a haircut, open a box of choco-
lates, or shop for a bathing suit. Instead, I make it a goal to
perk up and be happy. The best way is to become a "joy germ
carrier." Infecting people with joy so they break out in symp-
toms of laughter—that's the very best way to beat the blues.

I've made it a habit to wring out of every single day all the
fun and love I can find. If you don't know where to start the
next time you're feeling low, take it simply: Fill in the hours
with crazy excursions into comedy. You'll learn what makes
people laugh and how to communicate through chuckles. The
point is simply to get started. Never to give up. To be friendly
and to focus on the person next to you. People who like
people are people that people like![10]

BARBARA JOHNSON

FRIDAY

THE KEY TO FRIENDSHIP

Jesus said, "Love one another. As I have loved you, so you must love one another."

JOHN 13:34

The key to friendship between women—and somehow for us girls, it's not the easiest thing to achieve—is being able to accept each other unconditionally. If we can do that, the rewards are never-ending. And the pay dirt is definitely a bonanza! It's a proven that fact we will stay young longer, are less likely to be depressed, and will save a fortune in counseling fees!

The secret of friendship is that we bless each other, and within the blessing is a kaleidoscope of meaning—to make happy, to praise, to thank, to protect, to sanctify, to favor, to celebrate, to give benediction. It not only applies to best friends, but it applies to every cherished human relationship—husband and wife, parent and child, sister and brother, neighbor with neighbor, church member with church member. It's cross-cultural, cross-racial, cross-generational, and cross-backyardfence-ational—a made-up word, but that, too, is allowed with friends![11]

SUE BUCHANAN

WEEKEND

❋

A JOYFUL UP-LOOK

May the God of hope fill you with all joy
and peace as you trust in him.

ROMANS 15:13

No matter who you are, you have been made in God's image. Your life has eternal significance through Christ. Even in the most stable relationships, at times we can't be there for each other. But Christ will always be there. Christ is with you today as he was yesterday and will be tomorrow, and when you lay your head down for the last time, your life will be just beginning.

How can you trust? I encourage you to take a leap into the arms of the One who is able to fill your heart with love. Throw your fears to the wind. Christ did not come to remove all of our troubles, but to walk with us through every one of them. So, take a leap. Take a flying leap![12] He will catch you and never let you down.

SHEILA WALSH

Heavenly Father, thank you for always
being there for me. You are never too busy, and your
ears are always open to my cry. I leap into your arms
today and trust you with my whole heart. Amen.

MONDAY

HE LOVED YOU
ALL THE WAY TO THE CROSS

Jesus said, "God loved the world so much that
he gave his one and only Son."

JOHN 3:16 NIRV

What a lavish God we serve. His expressions of love and commitment to us are limitless. He keeps every promise he makes. His giving is never-ending. His love is unconditional. Faithful. "For I am convinced that neither death nor life, neither angels nor demons, neither the present nor the future, nor any powers, neither height nor depth, nor anything else in all creation, will be able to separate us from the love of God that is in Christ Jesus our Lord" (Romans 8:38–39).

Know how much he loves you this day. Don't mistake your ability to love or understand with his ability to love and understand. I suppose if you told Jesus, "I love you all the way to…" he would answer back that he loved you all the way to the cross—and that he'll continue to love you throughout eternity. It takes your breath away, and you can only respond with a heart of thankfulness.[13] We have much cause for rejoicing.

KATHY TROCCOLI

TUESDAY

DON'T SWEAT THE SMALL STUFF

Catch the foxes, the little foxes,
before they ruin our vineyard in bloom.

SONG OF SOLOMON 2:15 GNT

Psychiatrist Richard Carlson was on to something when he wrote:

When…we are irritated, annoyed, and easily bothered—our (over-) reactions not only make us frustrated but actually get in the way of getting what we want. We lose sight of the bigger picture, focus on the negative, and annoy other people who might otherwise help us. In short, we live our lives as if they were one big emergency! We often rush around looking busy, trying to solve problems, but in reality, we are often compounding them. Because everything seems like such a big deal, we end up spending our lives dealing with one drama after another. After a while, we begin to believe that everything really is a big deal. We fail to recognize that the way we relate to our problems has a lot to do with how quickly and efficiently we solve them.[14]

Now that you're more aware of what steals your joy, you can prepare yourself to guard it more effectively.[15]

TRACI MULLINS

WEDNESDAY

✦

HEARTS FULLY COMMITTED

Your hearts must be fully committed
to the LORD our God, to live by his decrees
and obey his commands, as at this time.

1 KINGS 8:61

Have you ever prayed for someone only to remember, right in the middle of your intercession, that you left the laundry in the washing machine yesterday?

For the Christian who commits his heart fully to the Lord, the devil employs a special weapon: distractions.

Thomas Kelly wrote, "The life that intends to be wholly obedient, wholly submissive, wholly listening, is astonishing in its completeness. Its joys are ravishing, its peace profound, its humility the deepest, its power world-shaking, its love enveloping, its simplicity that of a trusting child. It is the life and power of Jesus of Nazareth, who knew that 'when thine eye is single, wholly devoted, the whole body is also full of light.'"

"Give me an undivided heart, that I may fear your name" (Psalm 86:11).

Full-hearted commitment is no petty duty, no piecemeal performance made up of fragments of time. Wholehearted devotion involves the best of time for prayer, study, and worship.[16]

JONI EARECKSON TADA

THURSDAY

❋

GETTING INTO A PRAYING MOOD

*Let us come before his presence with thanksgiving
and make a joyful noise unto him with psalms.*

PSALM 95:2 KJV

To help my children and myself to get focused on how to deal with problems, I ask my children if they have listened to praise music before they called to tell me about their woes. If they haven't, I ask them to call back after they have—unless, of course, it's an emergency.

I believe one of the best ways to get in a praying mood is to listen to music that ushers you into a spirit of adoration. That, in turn, takes your mind off the problem and helps you to focus on the Problem-Solver.

While I wait for them to call back, I follow my own instructions. I sing, listen to gospel music, and pray. Usually, when they phone me again, both of us are in harmony with each other and with the Lord.

We are admonished to pray without ceasing because prayers assert God's power in our lives.[17] And when God's power is operating in our lives, we can't help but rejoice.

THELMA WELLS

FRIDAY

FACE YOUR FEARS

Caleb silenced the people before Moses and said,
"We should go up and take possession of the land,
for we can certainly do it."

NUMBERS 13:30

I have envisioned certain fears that I kept trying to keep ahead of, only to find that when I stopped and faced them, there really was nothing to fear after all. What I needed to do was quit trying to avoid them and face them instead.

After my husband died, I didn't think I could handle money matters like taxes, interest rates, and investments. I had no choice but to turn and face that fear. I would still rather deal with investments like they were broccoli, cauliflower, or grapefruit, but I have learned it won't leave me dead on the beach to read a tax form.

Facing fears with a prayer on my lips and faith in my heart allows me not only to trust God more but also to experience victory that comes from no one but him. Actually, that is a rather exhilarating way to stay fit[18] and be filled with joy.

MARILYN MEBERG

WEEKEND

JOY SAPPERS

You, O God, do see trouble and grief;
you consider it to take it in hand.

PSALM 10:14

N o matter what, don't ever let yesterday use up too much of today. If it sneaks up on you, turn the tables on it. Like interest rates, make trouble work for you, not against you. You don't always need a comedian to make you laugh. Once you get started, you can pull a few one-liners out of the bag yourself. When someone says, "Life is hard," say, "I prefer it to the alternative, don't you?" When somebody else complains about getting old, answer, "Right now, I'm just sitting here being thankful that wrinkles don't hurt!"

Life is too short to spend it being angry, bored, or dull. That was never God's intention. Maybe boredom and dullness aren't on any list of sins in the Bible, but they will sap your joy if you tolerate them.[19]

BARBARA JOHNSON

Heavenly Father, thank you for the precious life you've
given me. Remind me to live every moment to the fullest,
always seeing the good in each day, each person, each
circumstance. Thank you for the joy of being alive. Amen.

MONDAY

BE THERE FOR OTHERS

Two are better than one,
*   because they have a good return for their work:*
If one falls down,
*   his friend can help him up.*

ECCLESIASTES 4:9–10

We need each other. We're instructed to love, pray for, care about, accept, forgive, serve, encourage, and build up one another.

I love that about my partners in the Women of Faith conferences. We "be-bop" all over the country, watching out for each other. We serve one another joyfully. When one of us is down, we rally to her. When one celebrates, we rejoice together. We're a team. We never anticipated this kind of bonding, but bonded we are.

People need each other—no matter how much we insist we don't. Nobody is an island, an entity unto herself, or a Lone Ranger. We're in this thing called community, and part of the joy of community is sharing the weight—of burdens, losses, loneliness, and fear.

Look around. Who's there for you? And whom are you there for? Even those who insist they can make it on their own may be waiting for you to reach out and help. Even the Lone Ranger had a sidekick. [20]

LUCI SWINDOLL

TUESDAY

WHO IS THE CENTRAL FOCUS?

Jesus said,
"Everyone who exalts himself will be humbled,
and he who humbles himself will be exalted."

LUKE 18:14

Uppity is a downer. We are warned about thinking more highly of ourselves than we should. Like the time I thought I was lookin' good, only to discover that my pantyhose were streaming behind my foot as I sashayed through town.

Remember in Genesis when Joseph paraded his new coat for his brothers' viewing? They, in turn, stripped him of his colors and sold him into slavery. Thinking more highly of ourselves than we ought means a downfall is probably up ahead.

I guess God knew, that in order for Joseph to grow up, he would have to live down his need to be the center of attention. Here, though, is the amazing truth: Joseph grew to handle his down times as well as he did his up times.

Who is the central focus of our lives? The Lord? Or our need to be center stage? Are we willing, whether we ascend or descend, to be a shining example?[21] Only when Jesus is foremost in our minds can we know lasting joy.

PATSY CLAIRMONT

WEDNESDAY

❋

I Am Glad

I rejoiced with those who said to me,
*   "Let us go to the house of the LORD."*

PSALM 122:1

It's Sunday morning in Dallas. The airport routine—
check-in, baggage, security, and seating transfers—casts a
gray restlessness on my spirit. It was good to be here, but oh,
the joy of going home.

Ministering in foreign lands and worshiping with brothers
and sisters there is an experience I will always cherish. But I am
especially glad when I go to my own "house of the Lord." My
restless spirit finds a center, a refuge. The calendar, the traveling, the work—all of it becomes ordered when I'm home and
in my home church.

Are you glad when you go to church, your home church?
Can you bring your restlessness there? Do you find simple
pleasure in the people with whom you worship? I hope you do.
Cherish that which God has given as a centered rest for you.
Long for its weekly shelter, and rejoice in its heavenly promise
of rest.[22]

JONI EARECKSON TADA

THURSDAY

❋

A TOUCH OF BEAUTY

The LORD God made all kinds of trees grow
out of the ground—trees that were pleasing
to the eye and good for food.

GENESIS 2:9

I was driving down a familiar road one fall day when I almost drove off the road, the beauty was so intense. It looked as if God had sent in a team of the world's finest artists overnight. Every tree had changed to shades of deepest gold and robin red, to sun-kissed yellow and pumpkin orange. Leaves danced in the air and brushed against my windshield.

Notice the colors in your world! Look around your own home. How can you add a touch of beauty? Every one of us can do one small thing to add beauty to our workplace or kitchen or bedroom. File the papers cluttering the desk. Re-cover a pillow. Rearrange the furniture. Light a candle.

Maybe it's time for a new hairstyle or makeover. The makeup counters at the mall will give you a complimentary makeover with no obligation to buy. A friend tells me there's nothing like a professional shoeshine for lifting up a bad day. Open your eyes. Brighten your world.[23] Experience the joy.

SHEILA WALSH

FRIDAY

STRENGTH WHEN YOU NEED IT

*The Lord said to me, "My grace is sufficient for you,
for my power is made perfect in weakness."*

2 CORINTHIANS 12:9

My mother died of cancer. She showed amazing courage throughout her illness and handled the dying process with dignity and humility. She never once complained, only confessed that she was "getting tired." Before my eyes, she lived out the truth of one of her favorite phrases: "God will give you strength when you need it."

When I was in the middle of the most difficult times of my life, she would offer those tender words. Now, as I look back and see that God really was with me, giving me grace to bear the unbearable, I realize that my mother was right. More than that, I know she spoke the heart of God.

There is no situation in this life that he will not miraculously lead us through—giving us a strength and peace that we know is beyond anything we could conjure up. Lean on him. Abandon yourself to his grace. God will give you strength when you need it.[24] His love and joy will sustain you.

KATHY TROCCOLI

WEEKEND

❖

JOY COMES IN THE MORNING

Those who sow in tears
will reap with songs of joy.

PSALM 126:5

One night, Bill and I were listening to a pastor on the radio encouraging his congregation. With a heartfelt, genuine compassion, he kept repeating Psalm 30:5. "Weeping endures for the night!" he would say, "But joy comes in the morning! Let me hear you, now. Weeping endures for the night …"

With one great voice, they returned the affirmation, "Joy comes in the morning!"

As we listened, the problems in our own lives seemed to settle into perspective in the immense power of God and his great faithfulness.

No matter how tragic the circumstances, no matter how long the spiritual drought, no matter how dark the days, the dawn will come. We will know that our God has been there all along. We will hear him say, through it all, "Hold on, my child, joy comes in the morning!"[25]

GLORIA GAITHER

Heavenly Father, in the dark night of the soul,
you are with me. I sow in tears now, but I thank you
for bringing joy in the morning. Amen.

MONDAY

REMEMBERING WHEN

I will remember the deeds of the LORD;
  yes, I will remember your miracles of long ago....
You are the God who performs miracles.

PSALM 77:11, 14

Have you ever heard the phrase, "compare and despair"? That's what the Israelites did as God led them by Moses through the desert. Every time they found their circumstances wanting, they recalled the "good old days"—when they were slaves in Egypt! The comparison always led to despair. If their defective memory hadn't had such grave implications, their behavior would have been almost comical.

The psalmists had keen insight into this foible. That's why they gave so much press to recalling the days of old—not so we can moan and groan about what we think we've lost, but so we can rejoice in the undeniable record of God's faithfulness to his faithless people.

"Remembering when" can be one of the most effective tools we can use to restore our confidence in the God who never leaves or forsakes us. That's reason for rejoicing.[26]

TRACI MULLINS

TUESDAY

LET HIM LEAD YOU

*Since you are my rock and my fortress,
    for the sake of your name lead and guide me.*

PSALM 31:3

Sometimes we find ourselves wandering in a wilderness, lost and unable to find our way out. For years I felt that way. Nothing seemed to work. I felt stripped and anxious, unable to determine what my mission in life should be.

I didn't know how to set my sights on God and let him lead me.

It's true that goals help us to be disciplined and to aim our energies toward accomplishing what we've set out to do. But for me, setting goals and not leaning on God had led me into a perplexing and fretful place. I learned that first I needed to humbly go before God and give him my concerns. Then he would provide me with direction.

You may be in the same wilderness I was in, anxiously wandering around, fearful that disaster is headed toward you. Relinquish your anxieties to God, for he cares for you. Direction will come in God's good time.[27] Until then, let his joy fill you to overflowing and give you peace.

THELMA WELLS

WEDNESDAY

❋

SIMPLY BEING TOGETHER

They devoted themselves...to the fellowship,
to the breaking of bread and to prayer.

ACTS 2:42

Since Thanksgiving was only a day away, I hurried off to buy a frozen turkey, a sixteen-pound Jenny O.

The directions on Jenny's frozen back instructed me to place her in my refrigerator where she would thaw. With innocent anticipation, I pulled Jenny out of the refrigerator Thanksgiving morning. She wasn't as stiff as the day we had met, but she certainly wasn't soft and pliable.

Jenny crawled into my oven around eleven o'clock and came out around five in the evening. She was flavorful and moist until I cut more than an inch deep. Then we hit pink meat, which threw me into fits about salmonella poisoning and the like.

In spite of this, my family, some dear friends, and I had a wonderful time together. Sometimes I forget and allow myself to focus on the externals of a celebration, which, of course, throttles my internal experience of joy. Even if we had been reduced to ordering out for pizza, we would have had a great time, simply because we were together.[28]

MARILYN MEBERG

THURSDAY

❈

THE ESSENTIAL IS INVISIBLE

*The LORD said, "I do not look at the things people
look at. Man looks at how someone appears on
the outside. But I look at what is in the heart."*

1 SAMUEL 16:7 NIRV

How quickly we judge the outward appearance of other
people. We see clothes that don't match. We look at
the cars, manners, music, posture, or facial characteristics of
other people ... judging all the while.

If human perspective had been the criterion for God's judgment, the Swindolls would have been zapped long ago. My
brothers and I have lived most of our lives in well-worn clothes
that don't match. Often I go to the store in my oldest sweats—
I don't want to change clothes just to pick up a carton of milk.

In Antoine de Saint-Exupery's book, *The Little Prince*, he
states, "It is only with the heart that one can see rightly; what
is essential is invisible to the eye." This captures what we read
in Scripture. We have no right to pass judgment on other
people. When I don't put any judgmental demands on others,
I'm happiest, because I know I'm doing what is right. And
when nobody puts demands on me, it frees me to be who I
am.[29] My joy can be full.

LUCI SWINDOLL

FRIDAY

INTO THE LIGHT

This is the message we have heard
from him and declare to you: God is light;
in him there is no darkness at all.

1 JOHN 1:5

Sometimes I think we misinterpret faith. In my own life, instead of grabbing hold of what was wrong and dealing with it, no matter how painful it was, I acted as if everything was fine. But was I living by faith or by wishful thinking? Jesus never encouraged his friends to cover over pain, but He instructed them to bring it out into the light, where healing can be found. Yes, rejection may well happen, but bringing the pain to the light is still the best way to live.

Sometimes we simply don't want to face the truth about ourselves. Sometimes we do not seek help because it will mean we have to change, and change is painful and unpredictable. To me, now, faith is bringing all that is true about our lives into the blinding light of God's grace. It is believing that he will still be there at the end of the journey.[30] And even when the road is difficult, we can experience his joy as we walk in the light.

SHEILA WALSH

WEEKEND

❋

BOOMERANG JOY

The angel said,
"I bring you good news of great joy."

LUKE 2:10

Anytime we stop to be present with others in their trouble, we carry the opportunity to bring boomerang joy. You don't have to be famous or important. You don't have to be acclaimed or much sought after. Just be you. Stay true to yourself and to those values that keep you grounded in kindness.

Keep looking for the boomerang surprise in your life. Listen for the whirring sound that means it may be getting close. Always stay connected to people and seek out things that bring you joy. Dream with abandon. Pray confidently. But be careful what you pray for—because everything and anything is possible through the power of prayer![31]

BARBARA JOHNSON

Heavenly Father, I'm going to be on the lookout for joy
today. Give me opportunities to share the good news of
your love with others, to encourage them and point them
to you. Then I will watch for the blessings that will
boomerang back to me because you are so good. Amen.

MONDAY

A MEANINGFUL DESTINY

O LORD, our Sovereign, ... what are human beings that
you are mindful of them,
*   mortals that you care for them?*
Yet you have made them a little lower than God,
*   and crowned them with glory and honor.*

PSALM 8:1, 4–5 NRSV

David and the other psalmists seem stunned by the notion that a God "high up" in the heavens could care about what happens on this puny planet, but again and again God irrefutably proves it to them. A passage from Zephaniah in the old King James Version expresses it well: "The LORD thy God in the midst of thee is mighty; he will save, he will rejoice over thee with joy; he will rest in his love, he will joy over thee with singing" (3:17).

The Sovereign Lord of history allows people to exert an influence on him, just as he exerts influence on them. A desperate woman prays, and God sends a prophet; a disheartened old man refuses to curse God, and the impact reverberates throughout the cosmos. We exist not in a meaningless world, we do not act out some god's whim, but we exist to fulfill a meaningful Destiny ordained for us by a personal God.[32]

PHILIP YANCEY

TUESDAY

INVADING OTHERS' ORBITS

Clothe yourselves with compassion, kindness,
humility, gentleness and patience.

COLOSSIANS 3:12

I'm a Peter. At least in the sense that I've stepped, sometimes rushed, and yes, even hurled myself into others' orbits. Even lopped off a few ears (at least it probably felt like it to those involved). In fact, I remember far too clearly a situation some years ago in which I felt led to inform a dear woman of some of her character flaws (even though she had not asked). She was gracious, even though I had hurled myself into her orbit uninvited.

I know the Lord has forgiven me, but I don't want him to release me from the regret I feel. It serves as a sort of "orbital monitoring device," keeping me in my designated space. For I have found there is plenty for me to do in my own solar system without attempting adjustments in someone else's.

We need to respect others' space and clean up our own orbit. Then, one day, in the twinkling of an eye, we will be headed through space toward Home! What joy![33]

PATSY CLAIRMONT

WEDNESDAY

❖

SEEING THE FACE
OF JESUS IN OTHERS

Jesus said, "The King will reply, 'I tell you the truth, whatever you did for one of the least of these brothers of mine, you did for me.'"

MATTHEW 25:40

D irty. Hungry. They all look the same, lying on the sidewalk, park bench, or church steps. Some of us turn away in disgust and some in sympathy. I try to challenge myself to turn toward them, the way that Jesus would. Are these the faces of "soulless" people, or could they be the face of Christ?

The Bible acknowledges our ease at loving the lovely and our resistance to loving the unlovely. I believe that Christ is disguised in men today. May we be aware of his presence in humanity. May we be aware of his need in the needs of others. May we offer his love outside of the boundaries of our own love. May we never let our hearts become so numb and so blind that we cannot see the face of Jesus in the people we meet every day of our lives.[34] By loving others in this way, we will experience joy and fulfillment at a new, deeper level.

KATHY TROCCOLI

THURSDAY

✦

LEARNING TO BEND

I am convinced that neither death nor life, neither angels nor demons, neither the present nor the future, nor any powers, neither height nor depth, nor anything else in all creation, will be able to separate us from the love of God that is in Christ Jesus our Lord.

ROMANS 8:38–39

Once I watched a little boy playing on a huge weathered tree adrift at the lakeshore. The boy thought the waves on the lake were pulling the tree away from shore. He kept crying, "Daddy, Daddy, help, it's moving." I felt kind of sorry for the little guy because the rocking of the waves must have felt powerful to him. But his dad, who was standing a few feet away on the beach, knew that huge tree wasn't going anywhere. He was nearby. He expected his boy to take solace in that security.

I thought, *That's a lot like me and my heavenly Father.* God gives me credit for being able to take more than I think I can take. He wants me to take comfort in the fact that he is close. He isn't going anywhere, and no matter how scary things get, he won't come unglued. Our afflictions are designed not to break us, but to bend us toward the eternal and the holy. God sticks with us through it all. [35]

BARBARA JOHNSON

FRIDAY

❋

GOD'S PLAN

Those who know your name will trust in you,
for you, LORD, have never forsaken those who seek you.

PSALM 9:10

How do we truly give up our agendas? How do we genuinely say, "Not my will but yours, Lord"? For me, the answer to that question is found in my understanding and acceptance of God's sovereignty. God "works out everything in conformity with the purpose of his will." All happenings on this earth and in my life are worked out in conformity with his purpose—not mine, but his.

What softens my response to God's sovereignty is to remember that the nature of God is love. His love is simply too great and too all-encompassing to step around.

Based on that love platform is the realization that I am not incidental in the grand scheme of things. I am not an afterthought. God's love-inspired preplanning for each of us is not haphazard or impersonal. His timing may throw me, or his sovereign plan may even grieve me, but I am always sheltered in his sovereign hand. Such a joyful revelation![36]

MARILYN MEBERG

WEEKEND

❋

AN ETERNAL JOYFEST!

*Rejoice, inasmuch as ye are partakers of
Christ's sufferings; that, when his glory shall be revealed,
ye may be glad also with exceeding joy.*

1 PETER 4:13 KJV

As Christians, the ultimate boost to our joy is summed up by Jesus' words to his disciples shortly before he left them to ascend to his Father: "Now is your time of grief, but I will see you again and you will rejoice, and no one will take away your joy" (John 16:22). Jesus comforted his friends with these words as he prepared for death, and he fulfilled them when he appeared to several loved ones after his resurrection.

No matter what we go through on earth, our ultimate joy is guaranteed on the day we see Christ face-to-face, if we know him as our personal Savior and Lord. When we leave this world, we will join him—unless he comes back to get us before we've lived out our days (see Matthew 24:30–31, 42). Either way, we're in for an eternal joyfest![37]

TRACI MULLINS

*Heavenly Father, thank you for giving me joy
here on earth, and for the fullness of joy I will
experience when I see you face-to-face. Amen.*

Monday

He'll Make Music Through You

Jesus said, "Do not worry beforehand about what to say. Just say whatever is given you at the time, for it is not you speaking, but the Holy Spirit."

Mark 13:11

God draws people to himself. Each of us is just his mouthpiece on earth. Whether we say just the right thing or can't think of anything that seems right, all we have to do is open our mouths and trust God to use us. That doesn't mean we shouldn't be prepared to offer a reasonable explanation for our faith, but it does take the pressure off of us. We are the instruments, but God is the One who must make the music through us.

Have you tried to explain a spiritual principle to someone lately and sounded only sour notes? Have you been stymied about how to make clear that thing that seems so obvious to you? Remembering the difference between your role and God's role can help to comfort you if you've blown it. It may even give you the push you need to increase your knowledge so you can "sound off" more eloquently next time.[38] Allow the joy of being used by God to motivate you.

Thelma Wells

TUESDAY

NEVER CAGE JOY

You have made known to me the path of life;
you will fill me with joy in your presence,
with eternal pleasures at your right hand.

PSALM 16:11

A little girl set off to search for the bluebird of happiness. She looked in the past but couldn't find it. She looked to the future but couldn't find the bird. Then she looked in the present. When the bluebird of happiness appeared, she felt joyful. She felt inspired. She went out to do good while the bird sang a beautiful song in the treetops.

After a while, the little girl grew afraid. *What if I lose the bluebird of happiness?* she wondered. So she built a cage of bamboo sticks, filled it with seed and pretty branches, and tucked the bird away for safekeeping. But the bird grew quiet, singing less and less until it finally stopped altogether. Eventually, the bluebird of happiness died.

The little girl learned that joy can't be contained——it must be free to come and go, which it will——just as trouble is never permanent. I am determined never to cage joy if it alights on my shoulder. I will set the bluebird of happiness free to bless some other person's life.[39]

BARBARA JOHNSON

WEDNESDAY

❋

RUN TO GOD WHEN YOU'RE AFRAID

I trust in your unfailing love;
my heart rejoices in your salvation.
I will sing to the LORD,
for he has been good to me.

PSALM 13:5–6

In the Bible, fear is first mentioned in Genesis 3:10, when Adam said to the Lord, "I heard you in the garden, and I was afraid." Fear entered our world at the Fall. Adam was afraid because he knew he had disobeyed God. The peace and tranquility of the Garden of Eden was lost forever. Once humankind listened to the serpent, good and evil became players on our stage. From that point on in human history, fear either threw us on our faces before God or caused us to hide our faces from him.

David was very familiar with fear. In Psalm 56:3 he wrote, "When I am afraid, I will trust in you," and he cried out in Psalm 69:1, "Save me, O God, for the waters have come up to my neck."[40]

Fear robs us of the joy God means for us to experience. But when we follow David's example and run to the Father for refuge, God's love will drive out all fear.

SHEILA WALSH

THURSDAY

❁

HE'LL NEVER LET YOU DOWN

Many are the afflictions of the righteous,
*   but the LORD rescues them from them all.*

PSALM 34:19 NRSV

Christians sometimes have more trouble handling trouble than the world does, because we think we should be perfect. As things veer out of control, you may find yourself asking, "Who stopped payment on my reality check?"

Too often our faith is shallow. We cling to the padded cross instead of the "old rugged cross" of the hymn. What should set us apart is our trust, our ability to let God loose in our circumstances rather than forever trying to control them ourselves.

Admit it and save yourself years of worry. There are no superfamilies. There are no perfect people. You are right where "X" marks the spot on the map of life. Whatever dilemma you're facing, ask yourself what difference it will make one hundred years from today. The difference is in letting go and letting God. He'll never let you down. He'll help you face tomorrow with open hands, an open heart, an open mind, and tons of confidence.[41] His joy will be your strength.

BARBARA JOHNSON

FRIDAY

A JOYFUL SONG

Make a joyful noise to the LORD, all the earth;
break forth into joyous song and sing praises.

PSALM 98:4 NRSV

According to the psalms, praise need not always be sober and reflective. The psalmists praised God with sensuous abandon, and as a result, their worship services may well have resembled a modern pep rally more than a sedate symphony concert. "Sing for joy! Shout aloud!" they command. Musical instruments in those days included cymbals, tambourines, trumpets, rams' horns, harps, and lyres. Sometimes dancing erupted. In the psalmist's imagination, the world could not contain the delight God inspired. The psalms wonderfully provide the necessary words. We merely need to enter into those words, letting the content of the psalms realign our inner attitudes.

When the ancient Hebrews encountered something beautiful or majestic, their natural response was not to contemplate the scene or to analyze it, but rather to praise God for it and maybe even write a poem. Their fingers itched for the harp; their vocal cords longed for the hymn. Praise, for them, was joy expressing itself in song and speech, an "inner health made audible," in C.S. Lewis's phrase.[42]

PHILIP YANCEY

WEEKEND

❋

EPITAPHS

Who is wise and understanding among you?
Let him show it by his good life, by deeds done
in the humility that comes from wisdom.

JAMES 3:13

Most of us won't have the prerogative to write our own epitaph. It will be written by someone else—someone who will seek to capture a single phrase that epitomizes our entire life. If you were to die today, what phrase would capture your essence? What words would characterize you?

The Creator has made us each one of a kind. There is nobody else exactly like us, and there never will be. Each of us is his special creation and alive for a distinctive purpose. Because of this, the person we are, and the contribution we make by being that very person, are vitally important to God. That makes me want to be today exactly who God made me to be, and no one else.[43]

LUCI SWINDOLL

Heavenly Father, thank you for skillfully crafting me
in my mother's womb with my own unique set of gifts and
talents. Help me to develop them to the fullest, so that
others will receive the maximum benefit from them.
May everything I am bring glory to you. Amen.

MONDAY

YOU WILL LAUGH AGAIN

A time to kill and a time to heal,
   a time to tear down and a time to build,
a time to weep and a time to laugh,
   a time to mourn and a time to dance.

ECCLESIASTES 3:3–4

When the Israelites were carried into captivity in Babylon, Psalm 137 says that they sat down by the river and wept. God was still on the throne, but his people were in pain. I wonder sometimes if we think it ungodly to mourn the changing seasons of life, as if doing so were to question God's wisdom. I do not believe that expressing the pain we feel diminishes God or our faith in him. Everything in our lives comes to us through the gracious hands of the Lord, but that does not mean our lives will be free of pain. In fact, we are told that life will include hurt and hard times.

If we do not tear down, we can never lastingly build. If we do not take time to mourn, we will have no joy in dancing; and if we do not weep, we will never be swept away with laughter. Jesus said: "Blessed are you who weep now, for you will laugh" (Luke 6:21).[44]

SHEILA WALSH

TUESDAY

YIELD, SO HE CAN ACT

Strengthen your feeble arms and weak knees.
"Make level paths for your feet," so that the lame
may not be disabled, but rather healed.

HEBREWS 12:12–13

O ur capacity to feel, think, and experience is so great—
to taste the sweetness of joy that life can bring, to bask
in the peace of God, to worship on the mountaintops, to ride
high on loving and being loved. All of these are wonderful and
precious gifts, and I'm so thankful for them.

But oh, the downfall when we rely on these experiences
as the truth or believe in them as the absolute. For when the
sweetness goes sour, the storm comes raging in, the dryness
hits, or the loneliness prevails, we must continually remember
that God's truth never changes. My feelings change, my circumstances change, but the truth never does. I *must* push
beyond it all and make a choice—to have faith, to go on, to lift
my drooping hands, to strengthen my weak knees, and to
make a straight path for my feet. As I yield, he can act, and he
will act. Then yes, what is lame—hopelessness, doubt, fear,
anger, bitterness, insecurity—can be healed.[45]

KATHY TROCCOLI

WEDNESDAY

❖

WHERE ARE YOU?

*Jesus Christ is the same yesterday
and today and forever.*

HEBREWS 13:8

How do we find the joy of God's presence? He is in our prayers guiding our words, he is in our songs as we worship him, and he is filling our mouths when we comfort a friend or speak wisdom to someone who needs hope. Sometimes we can search so hard for the miraculous that we miss the obvious reality of his ever-present nearness. Count your blessings. He is in them, too.

We can't command the Lord into our awareness. He is King; we are his beloved subjects. When our hearts are tenderly responsive and it suits his greater plan, then the Lord will lift the thin veil that separates us. And we will be stunned to realize that he has been closer than our own breath all along.

By the way, it has been my experience that I keep refinding him, which has helped to define me. You, too, may lose track of your faith. Remember, it is never too late to step back on the path to abundant joy.[46]

PATSY CLAIRMONT

THURSDAY

✸

DELEGATE!

*"Choose men of ability from all of the people.
They must have respect for God. You must be able to
trust them.... Appoint them as officials over thousands,
hundreds, fifties and tens. Let them serve the people."*

EXODUS 18:21–22 NIRV

One of the most rewarding ways to relate to others is to give them ownership over what's going on. At home, the entire family should share in keeping things up around the house. At work, people want to be a part of things and to have responsibility with accountability. And others in your life are waiting for you to take some items off your calendar so that they can put them on theirs.

It takes awhile to complete the delegation process. Training, explaining, and overseeing are all part of it. However, when everyone has been given tasks and can do them with little supervision, you begin to reap the results.

I hypothesize that you have some people to whom you can delegate housework, office work, and church work. Trust people enough to give them important tasks. Delegate.[47] Then rejoice!

THELMA WELLS

FRIDAY

CRACKED POTS
AND TARNISHED VESSELS

We have this treasure in earthen vessels,
that the surpassing greatness of the power
may be of God and not from ourselves.

2 CORINTHIANS 4:7 NASB

Eve was an earthen vessel in the truest form, a one-and-only woman if ever there was one. Unable or unwilling to resist the enemy's fruity fling, she lost the sweetness of her highest calling. Even though Eve was unique, her sin made her common…as does ours.

Sin tarnishes our one-of-a-kind brilliance. I have a copper pot that quickly dulls when not tended to. It has to be cleaned and polished regularly. We also lose our individual luster and become no more than common pots when we are tainted by sinful behavior.

All we cracked pots and tarnished vessels need to heed the lesson Eve taught us and strive to keep our individual containers shipshape.

If you're feeling tarnished, ask God to polish you with his love and forgiveness. Don't let sin steal the joy that comes when your earthen vessel is its sparkling best.[48]

PATSY CLAIRMONT

WEEKEND

❋

PEACE DANCING

Though you have not seen him, you love him; and even though you do not see him now, you believe in him and are filled with an inexpressible and glorious joy.

1 PETER 1:8

I t is not possible to always be happy. It is possible to always have the joy of the Lord. Some have described it as a calm-centeredness that tickles at the edges. It's a solid assurance that laughs if given the chance. It is unwavering confidence that can't help but look on the bright side. It's God's gift to you—the external expression of a heart in relationship with God. My friend Tim Hansel once said that joy is peace dancing.

Think of all the things that make up the joy of the Lord, and your smile can't help but last.[49]

JONI EARECKSON TADA

Heavenly Father, thank you for the wonderful gift of your joy. No matter what is going on around me, my heart can dance with your joy and peace, knowing that you have everything under control. Cause your joy in me to be a beacon of light to draw the sorrowful, hopeless, and depressed to you. Amen.

MONDAY

CHOOSE TO REIN IN FEAR

The LORD is my strength and my shield;
my heart trusts in him, and I am helped.
My heart leaps for joy
and I will give thanks to him in song.

PSALM 28:7

To David, fear was a reaction to forces that were coming against him; it was not a response, not a way of life. As an older man, he was able to deal with fear and the threats of his enemies because of how he had lived as a young man. David had been a shepherd boy, whose job was to make sure no harm came to the sheep. Lions or bears would try to carry a lamb away, but David was right there, slingshot in hand, ready to fight for the lamb's life. In his early years, while hidden away in a field, he made the choices to become the man he would later be. If David had run away as a boy, he would have run away as an adult; instead, he grabbed hold of his fear and reined it in.[50]

Choose today to rein in fear, knowing that the Lord is your strength and shield. Your heart will leap with joy as you put your trust in him.

SHEILA WALSH

TUESDAY

❋

HE ANSWERS WHEN YOU CALL

You will call, and the LORD will answer;
* you will cry for help, and he will say: Here am I.*

ISAIAH 58:9

At the call center in Denver International Airport, each of the thirty-six operators may answer as many as 260 calls per day. Then they relay messages to some of the ninety-thousand passengers and others that pass through the concourses within any twenty-four-hour period.

Sometimes the messages are frantic, such as one from a daughter who helped her father carry his luggage to the check-in counter for his trip to Bangkok and then returned to the parking lot to discover a major problem. That's when the call center might relay a message begging, "Don't get on that plane! You have Sarah's only set of car keys in your pocket!"

When I read about these relayed messages, I chuckled, but then I thought of how fortunate we are that when we need to get an urgent message to our Father in heaven, we don't have to route our plea through a busy call center.[51] He is always there to listen when we call.

BARBARA JOHNSON

WEDNESDAY

❋

JOY BEYOND THIS WORLD

*All Scripture is God-breathed and is useful
for teaching, rebuking, correcting and training
in righteousness, so that the man of God may
be thoroughly equipped for every good work.*

2 TIMOTHY 3:16–17

What difference do ancient prophetic visions make to those of us stuck in this fallen world? They awaken in us what we hope to ultimately be true. Would it make a difference for any of us to know that God is indeed a God of justice and peace and hope, no matter how this world appears?

The prophets call us to a vision of a deeper, underlying reality, to "joy beyond the walls of the world, more poignant than grief" (as J.R.R. Tolkien wrote). By giving a glimpse of the future, and of the cosmic present, they make it possible for us to believe in a just God, after all. Justice is essential to the prophets, for God's reputation rides on whether he can ultimately deliver justice to this world. Like a bell tolling from another world, the prophets proclaim that no matter how things now appear, there is no future in evil, only in good.[52]

PHILIP YANCEY

THURSDAY

❉

VISION AND FAITH

It is God who works in you to will
and to act according to his good purpose.

Vision is when you see it and others don't. Faith is when you do it and others won't. With vision and faith, things can be done.

One of the greatest byproducts of believing in something, and then going for it, is joy. I've often said, "My favorite thing in life is doing something new while having a good time." That's the essence of joy.

Perhaps you have an idea of something you would like to do, but you're scared. You've never done anything like it before. Maybe the idea just won't go away. But it's outside your comfort zone, and you don't feel adequate for the task. Pray, *Lord, if this desire is from you, will you bring it to pass? Help me know where to start.*

And then start. This is the faith part. Work hard. Do what makes sense to you. Ask the Lord whom to talk to who might help you. Talk with them.

What has he given you the desire to do? You can do it.[53]

LUCI SWINDOLL

FRIDAY

CURVES AHEAD

There is no fear in love. But perfect love
drives out fear, because fear has to do with punishment.
The one who fears is not made perfect in love.
We love because God first loved us.

1 JOHN 4:18–19

L ife is full of curves—sometimes gentle, pleasant, and surprisingly gratifying curves, and sometimes curves that threaten to overwhelm me in their sharpness. The seat-belt ensuring my survival is this one profound and simple truth: Jesus loves me.

This assurance is crucial as I ride out the curves on my journey. If I'm unsure of his love, I tend to either think the curves are clear evidence that I'm not one of the favored ones or that he wants to use the curves to punish me for something. That's why the truth of his love is so liberating. It softens me, it satisfies me, and it serves as a salve for my bleeding soul.

So when the road sign *Curves Ahead* pops up in your life, tighten the seatbelt of his love and remember that he is strong and capable of using his strength on your behalf—sometimes in the most amazing ways.[54]

MARILYN MEBERG

WEEKEND

❁

I HAVE A FLASHLIGHT

The people walking in darkness
have seen a great light;
on those living in the land of the shadow of death
light has dawned.

ISAIAH 9:2

I am a believer in Jesus and his promises: If the sun doesn't shine, I have a flashlight—his Word, which is a lamp unto my feet, guiding me every step; his eyes, seeing for me when I am too blind to see for myself; his fire, setting my heart ablaze so that I can see my sin and allow his love to consume it. The sweet glow of his presence shines into my darkness. And as I have received, I can give; I can hold out my flashlight, enabling others to see and be comforted when the sun is not shining and the days are like nights in their lives.

We must not sit in the dark. We must remember what we have in him. His light and his love are ever shining.[55] Because of it, our hearts are filled with joy.

KATHY TROCCOLI

Heavenly Father, thank you for being the light in my darkness.
Shine on my circumstances, so I can see things the way
you see them. Use me to light the way for others. Amen.

Monday

Don't Quit

Do not throw away your confidence; it will be richly rewarded. You need to persevere so that when you have done the will of God, you will receive what he has promised.

HEBREWS 10:35–36

Defying odds, breaking barriers, not being held back. I know people like that. They're a source of encouragement to me. They hang tough when others give up, forge ahead when others lag behind, choose to be cheerful when others sink in defeat.

Yet even more powerful are the words of Jesus, who challenged his followers to move mountains, walk on water, and prepare a picnic for five thousand. He assured us we would do no less than the impossible.

I don't know the circumstances of your life. Maybe you're experiencing a financial crisis, a relational struggle, or a genuine feeling of inadequacy. Whatever your biggest problems, be sure you aren't surrendering to the odds.

Don't quit, my friend. Push ahead to the joy of accomplishment. You have the whole sky above your head and God by your side.[56]

LUCI SWINDOLL

TUESDAY

FORGIVEN

*God says: "I will forgive their wickedness
and will remember their sins no more."*

JEREMIAH 31:34

How often do we ignore God's rules for our lives because we're too busy, are too involved in our own thing, don't believe, make up our own rules, or choose to be downright rebellious? I can imagine God looking at us and saying, "My children, how many times does it take to convince you that my way is the right way? My timing is the perfect timing? My authority is the ultimate authority? My instructions will lead you to a way that has been designed for your good. Why don't you obey me?"

As he questions us, if we're sensitive to listen to his admonishment, we're quick to say, "Father, I'm sorry!" Before the twinkling of an eye, he says, "Forgiven!"

Hallelujah, we don't have to listen to all that fussing! He knows when we mean what we say, and He is ready, willing, and able to forgive to the utmost without our having to talk and talk and talk about what we have done wrong. Praise God for the power in the phrase, "I'm sorry!"[57]

THELMA WELLS

WEDNESDAY

✦

ETERNAL GOOD

*We know that in all things God works
for the good of those who love him.*

ROMANS 8:28 NIRV

To God, life is a process—not a means to an end, but the goal. Whatever sends us running to him, makes us embrace him, causes us to depend on him, is the best good in our lives.

At times, we have been so full of gratitude and awe that we haven't been able to do anything else but sing, "Let's just praise the Lord." At other times we haven't been able to see how God could possibly be there in our dark circumstances, yet we have learned that he was always—in all things—up to something good in our lives. That "good" is always eternal good.

Some of life's circumstances seem senseless, and others, too painful to bear. But when we base our confidence on a perspective broader than this world's view, we can trust that what our sovereign God is working to accomplish is making our circumstances the servant of his purposes.

Let's just praise the Lord![58]

GLORIA GAITHER

Thursday

❋

Memories

This I call to mind
and therefore I have hope.

LAMENTATIONS 3:21

My sweetest memories are the ones that inspire hope. And many of these memories are of life before my accident. I recall the grating sensation of a nail file against the tips of my fingers, and the sound of my nails tapping cool, ivory piano keys. I can still "feel" my fingers plucking the tight nylon string of my old guitar, touching peach fuzz, digging under an orange skin and peeling it. So many of my freshest memories have to do with my hands.

Why would memories like these inspire hope? They remind me that one day soon I'll have new hands. Fingers that will work and feel again, touch and pluck and pick and scrub and dig. Hands that will embrace loved ones.

Let your memories be your handhold on heaven. Do you have memories of better times, happier days? Use those to help you look forward to the day when God will wipe away every tear, when sorrow and sighing will be no more, and when joy will overtake you.[59]

JONI EARECKSON TADA

FRIDAY

YOU'RE A STAR!

*Those who are wise will shine like the brightness
of the heavens, and those who lead many
to righteousness, like the stars for ever and ever.*

DANIEL 12:3

Have you noticed how Americans have gone star struck?
Our appetite to know more about the lives of the rich
and famous seems to be insatiable. Talk shows, news pro-
grams, women's and even news magazines seem to be moving
farther from true journalism and more toward fluff about the
famous.

Did you ever wonder what it would be like to be a star?
Well, you are one! You are God's kingdom star. You may be
overweight, sport age spots, or find a new crinkle in your
face now and then. None of that matters, for your beauty is
generated from the inside. Stars don't merely reflect the
light of the sun like the moon does. Stars are little suns; they
generate their own light.

In heaven, we'll realize the true brilliance and beauty of
our lives. Although you may feel like insignificant stardust
here on earth, remember: You're a star. Live like one![60]

BARBARA JOHNSON

WEEKEND

❋

THE NATURE OF PRAISE

*I will give thanks to the LORD because of his righteousness
and will sing praise to the name of the LORD Most High.*

PSALM 7:17

According to C.S. Lewis, the writers of the psalms keep encouraging us to join them in praising the Lord. They are saying, "Look, I just have to show you.... God is so great, you just have to praise him with me." Lewis also said, "I used to think of praise in terms of giving a compliment of approval or the giving of honor. But it's more than that. We praise the things we value, the things we enjoy. It's a spontaneous overflow. We can't help but praise what we value."[61]

I love Jesus. I enjoy and value the Lord Jesus. My delight in praising him is an expression of what I feel. That's the nature of praise.[62]

JONI EARECKSON TADA

*Father God, I will come upon many reasons to
praise you each day. Give me the ability to see them
for what they are and take time to enjoy them.
Help me to make praise my second nature. Amen.*

MONDAY

CHOCOLATE-CHIP HUMOR

God will yet fill your mouth with laughter
and your lips with shouts of joy.

JOB 8:21

Human beings thrive on laughter. Since most of us can't afford vacations in Hawaii, we have to learn to make our own fun! The best way to do that is to keep your state of mind green and golden: Find, recycle, or produce joy wherever and however you can. A good humorist is a work of heart! The Hasidic Jews believe that the best way to worship God is by being happy. They even incorporate dance and celebration into their spiritual walk.

Humor, laughter, and fun are the chocolate chips in the ice cream of life. Remember the old-time "Good Humor man," who drove his ice-cream truck down every street in the neighborhood, chiming a jingle on those hot summer days? All the kids came running as soon as they heard the sound. But good humor doesn't drive down many streets anymore. You have to go out and look for it yourself.

Fortunately, it's not that hard to find.[63]

BARBARA JOHNSON

TUESDAY

FIRST-LINE DEFENSE

I will bless the LORD at all times:
his praise shall continually be in my mouth.

PSALM 34:1 KJV

When it comes to a final defense against the devil's attacks, we often bypass praise, and we scramble to *do* something—anything—to remedy, rectify, or resolve the problem. Make lists, set goals, get counseling, go shopping, raid the fridge, read a book on the subject, or talk about it with others. But praise? Yes—praise must always be our first line of defense.

Try memorizing, if you haven't already, the doxology:
Praise God from whom all blessings flow;
Praise Him all creatures here below;
Praise Him above, ye heavenly host;
Praise Father, Son, and Holy Ghost.

Now say it! Sing it in the shower as you start your day. Think about it while you're waiting in line…at the fast-food drive-in, the bank window, or the grocery store checkout. Say it at the dinner table to replace your usual blessing for the food. New joy will soon spring up in you, and the devil will be on the run.[64]

JONI EARECKSON TADA

WEDNESDAY

❋

MAKING MEMORIES

Look to the LORD and his strength;
  seek his face always.
Remember the wonders he has done.

PSALM 105:4–5

Remembering is important to God. He encourages us to make memories. In Joshua 3–4, we read the account of the Israelites moving the ark of the covenant across the flooded Jordan River. After the water parted to allow the ark and the Israelites to cross, God commanded the leaders of the twelve tribes to each take one stone from the river and to place it where the priests had stood with the ark when they arrived safely on the other shore. "These stones are to be a memorial to the people of Israel forever" (Joshua 4:7). They are still there today.

We're encouraged to remember the days of old, the wonders of God, the Sabbath, God's deeds and our struggles, our Creator, our youth, and that life is short. Surround yourself with whatever it takes to be reminded. God is faithful. Don't ever forget that.[65] It will keep your joy alive.

LUCI SWINDOLL

THURSDAY

❋

AN OPEN BOOK

You yourselves are our letter, written on our hearts,
known and read by everybody.

2 CORINTHIANS 3:2

I am often amazed at how I see my brothers and sisters representing Jesus to a world so in need of him. As I talk about Christianity to people, it's hard for me to refute some of the criticisms. I'm challenged and often find that I have to climb over many stereotypes.

We must do away with evangelistic rules. We must strive to hear the Lord and be the Lord in our everyday lives—and he may look different and sound different according to the needs of those around us. God wants to give his life to people.

Let the world hear him through your voice, see him in your eyes, touch him through your touch, and find him in the treasures of your heart. May we be a book others can't put down until they, too, have put their life and soul into the hands of God.[66] Then, with all of heaven, we can rejoice over our new brothers and sisters born into the kingdom.

KATHY TROCCOLI

FRIDAY

THE ROAD TO JOY

I do not consider myself yet to have taken hold of it. But one thing I do: Forgetting what is behind and straining toward what is ahead.

PHILIPPIANS 3:13

My daughter Vikki, with her free spirit, discovered that once you start to climb a mountain, it's so steep and rough that your only option is to keep your sights on finishing and your mind on the rocks and boulders up ahead. You have to keep looking forward and not back, and you have to pray every step of the way that you will make it.

The road to glory is difficult, with its rocks and boulders, its strain and struggle. Things aren't always as easy as we would like. Surprises and pitfalls wait for us along the road of life. We're going to sweat and sway and wonder why things are the way they are.

But every road has an end; every mountain has its peak. If you can just hold on and keep climbing, knowing that God is aware of how you're straining, he will bring you up and over the mountains, until you reach the joy that lies on the other side.[67]

THELMA WELLS

WEEKEND

❋

A MOUTHFUL OF PRAISE

My mouth is filled with your praise,
declaring your splendor all day long.

PSALM 71:8

P raise is not something we should be forced to do.
Rather, it should be the supernatural, effervescent
response of the born-again creature preparing itself for
heaven. The crowning glory of praise is to lose ourselves and
yet find ourselves in God. This is pure praise.

Has your mouth ever been filled to overflowing with
praise? Saturate yourself this week with God's Word. Recount
to him often the wonders of his creation. Muse and brood
over his death for you on the cross. Recall the remarkable
details of his glorious resurrection, and imagine the home he
has prepared for you in heaven. Before long, out of you will
flow that river of living water, gushing out in a torrent and
springing up to him in a joyous fountain of praise.[68]

JONI EARECKSON TADA

Heavenly Father, quicken me with a spirit of praise. Fill
my mouth with praises for you today and every day. Amen.

Monday

God's Glad Welcome

We may approach God with freedom and confidence.

Ephesians 3:12

There are moments in the harsh bleakness of winter that would be unbearable if there were not, tucked deep within its bosom, the promise of spring. But spring always comes. Dark moments in our hearts are mitigated only in the light of God's sovereignty. We must learn to draw upon the resources of a sovereign God—One who unreservedly offers us not solutions, not answers, not happy-ever-after endings, but his glad welcome—the assurance of his presence with us.

The desert has its edge, and in God's timing, the darkness will give way to light. Assured of his glad welcome, we can take our places in a world full of people like ourselves—people who don't know where to turn, who never in a million years expected to find themselves in their present circumstances—people for whom there are no answers but Jesus Christ. And we can do it joyfully![69]

JOY MacKENZIE

TUESDAY

THE IMAGE OF GOD

God created humankind in his image,
in the image of God he created them;
male and female he created them.

GENESIS 1:27 NRSV

Remember the scene in which a crowd of religious men threw a woman at Jesus' feet. She had been caught in adultery, and by law she should have been stoned to death. Jesus said, "If that is how you want to handle this, then let's spray everyone with the same dye. If you have never sinned, feel free to throw the first stone." Slowly the crowd slipped away. Jesus picked the woman up and said, "No one is left to accuse you, and neither do I—but don't do this anymore; you are worth more than this." (I have paraphrased this story from John 8.)

Christ recognized that every human being has been created in the image of God. Talk show hosts and their nutty guests, women who stream in to abortion clinics, gay rights activists, *must* be treated with dignity and respect, because the mark of the image of God rests upon us all.[70]

On everyone you meet, picture the face of Jesus and experience the joy in valuing others.

SHEILA WALSH

WEDNESDAY

❋

ME, MYSELF, AND I

God saw all that he had made, and it was very good.

GENESIS 1:31

Who am I? Me. I'm myself. No other. No duplicate. No clone. God created me, and I'm who he wants me to be. Nothing more. Nothing less. Nothing else. That's true for you, as well.

The writer of Job says that each of us has been uniquely shaped by God's hand. He has formed us exactly. The great I Am made us and shaped us. A blessed thought! I don't have to be anybody but me. And as I walk with Christ, he's in the process of making me more like himself. God created us into who we are and "nothing is to be rejected" (1 Timothy 4:4).

Being who you are can be difficult if you don't like who you are. Accept yourself as God's wonderful creation. Then you are free to be you without fear.

Who are you? God's unique creation. There's nobody just like you. Never has been, never will be. Only you can be you. Be who God made you to be.[71]

LUCI SWINDOLL

THURSDAY

❋

A LAUGHING FIRE

If the LORD doesn't build a house,
the work of its builders is useless.

PSALM 127:1 NIRV

Ruth Graham, wife of evangelist Billy Graham, titled one of her books *Come Sit by My Laughing Fire*. When I saw that title, I thought, *Yes, that's it!* The laughing fire is one that sputters with joy while it burns away the troubles of the day.

God wants you to build a laughing fire on the hearth of your heart. Use the fuel of his love to turn trouble into heat and energy for yourself and other people. Stoke the smoldering embers of your passion for life. As the smoke curls from the chimney, other people will be drawn to the sweet aroma of compassion.

Is there an inviting glow and a heavenly scent to your life? Invite the Lord into it. He'll make it a place of divine mystery and glory that will provide a safe haven for others as they pass by on their own journey toward him.[72]

BARBARA JOHNSON

FRIDAY

SHOUT HALLELUJAH!

Burst into songs of joy together,
* you ruins of Jerusalem,*
for the LORD has comforted his people,
* he has redeemed Jerusalem.*

ISAIAH 52:9

Hallelujah!" the chorus cries out at last, and from there the music soars into what is unarguably the most famous portion of Handel's *Messiah*, and one of the most jubilant passages of music ever composed. Handel himself said that when he wrote the Hallelujah Chorus, "I did think I did see all Heaven before me, and the Great God himself." When King George the First heard the Hallelujah Chorus at the London premiere in 1742, he, the nation's sovereign, stood to his feet in amazement, and audiences have honored his respectful tribute ever since.

Some skeptics suggest that King George stood to his feet less out of respect than out of the mistaken assumption that Handel's *Messiah* had reached its conclusion with the Hallelujah Chorus. Even today, novices in the audience make the same mistake. Who can blame them? After two hours of performance, the music seems to come to a point of culmination in the exuberant Chorus. What more is needed?[73]

PHILIP YANCEY

WEEKEND

FACE TO FACE

Show me your face,
  let me hear your voice;
for your voice is sweet,
  and your face is lovely.

SONG OF SONGS 2:14

God thinks your soul is beautiful when you praise him. That should make you want to praise him in word and with singing all the more.

It makes me feel like I can hardly wait to see his face. Like any bride-in-waiting, I find it hard to rest comfortably when I cannot see the face of the one I adore. When it comes to brides and bridegrooms, full intimacy comes between a man and woman when they are face to face. And when the Bible speaks of longing for God, it speaks in terms of wanting to see his face. The psalmist pleads with God, "Make your face shine upon us" (Psalm 80:3), and, "Do not hide your face from me" (Psalm 27:9). Ultimately, "in righteousness I will see your face; when I awake, I will be satisfied with seeing your likeness" (Psalm 17:15). What incredible joy it will be to hold the gaze of God.[74]

JONI EARECKSON TADA

Heavenly Father, I do long to see your face,
for there is none like you. I worship you for who you are,
the one true God, the living God. Amen.

MONDAY

STOP AND CONSIDER

I have learned to be content whatever the circumstances.

PHILIPPIANS 4:11

One day I decided to count all the projects I had in my house (things I could make with my hands). These might be kits or models, or patterns for designs to be created out of paper, yarn, wood, or clay—projects I had started and then left behind to pursue something else. When I finished counting, I figured I had seven years' worth of projects. I don't even know if I'll live that long!

Why do we so often feel that "there's something better out there"? I believe we're often uncomfortable with ourselves, so we go outside of ourselves in search of someone, or something, or some place that will bring us contentment. We want to be somebody else, somewhere else, doing something else, and truthfully, we will settle for almost anything.

The key to contentment is to *consider*. Consider who you are, and be satisfied with that. Consider what you have, and be satisfied with that. Consider what God is doing in your life, and be satisfied with that. You will be amazed at how much more comfortable you'll feel with yourself.[75]

LUCI SWINDOLL

TUESDAY

AN INCREDIBLE PARADOX

You must get rid of your old way of life. That's because it is polluted by longing for things that lead you down the wrong path. You were taught to be made new in your thinking. You were taught to start living a new life.

EPHESIANS 4:22–24 NIRV

To understand who I am without God and what I'm capable of without Jesus is so sobering. I'm easily subject to passions, lusts, lies, idols, sin, and death. At the same time, I know who I am in Jesus: a conqueror, a child of God, a sinner saved by grace, a receiver of the gift of heaven.

Internal voices tell me I look horrible, fat, and unattractive, and that I always will. When I listen to these blows to my self-esteem, I let them crush my ability to see the truth of who God says I am, all he says I will become, all he desires of me, and all that he has promised me. I am beautiful, lovely, and radiant *only* when I look to him, *only* when I listen to his words and what he says about me. When, through obedience, I allow his character to become my character, he fills and covers all the holes of my insecurity.[76] It frees my heart to rejoice and be glad.

KATHY TROCCOLI

WEDNESDAY

❋

SPIRITUAL WHITE-OUT

God said,
"I will forgive their wickedness
and will remember their sins no more."

HEBREWS 8:12

Sometimes we'd like to cancel God's appointments for us: Why must we go through this particular trial? Look this particular way? Be saddled with this particular thorn in the flesh? We'd like to reschedule some of our afflictions for another day, put off our troubles until a more convenient time. Often we try, but usually we find ourselves in a bigger mess than ever.

Always when things go wrong because we struggle against the way things are, God comes along to white-out our sin of rebellion. Our lack of faith. Unforgiveness. Complacency. That one little bottle does it all.

So, settle into the grace of his presence right now. He knows your name. It is written in his book. He knows all the days appointed for you. And you can bet on it; he knows how to use the white-out for his glory and your great good. Then he writes in the clean space the name of the One through whom you have been made righteous: Jesus Christ.[77]

BARBARA JOHNSON

THURSDAY

❖

JOY IS THE REAL THING

Surely you have granted him eternal blessings
and made him glad with the joy of your presence.

PSALM 21:6

Like many women, I have bags of costume jewelry. Each piece looks pretty for a while, but then it begins to fade, peel, or break. If you wear it in water long enough, it will turn your skin green. That's the trouble with happiness; it looks good, but it doesn't last.

But joy—that's the genuine article. Joy gives me calm assurance even though I go through the valley of the shadow of death. Joy enables me to hold my peace when people say and do ugly things to me. When I'm going through troubles, afflictions, persecution, danger, illness, and distress, when the enemy comes to steal, kill, and destroy, the joy in my heart shines even brighter. And joy is permanent. There may be times when it's overshadowed by human frailties, but unlike happiness, joy lasts for eternity.[78]

Are you relying on happiness rather than joy? Just like with jewelry, the authenticity has to do with the source. Joy can be obtained only through a relationship with God.

THELMA WELLS

FRIDAY

A PRESCRIPTION FOR JOY

A cheerful heart is good medicine,
  but a crushed spirit dries up the bones.

PROVERBS 17:22

When God said a joyful heart is good medicine, I believe that he was literal in his meaning.

A researcher named Jonathan Leake has discovered how a group of life-enhancing chemicals are triggered by laughter. These hormones are so powerful, they can energize a person's entire immune system and help it ward off diseases, including the common cold or the flu.

Arthur Stone, a professor of psychoneural immunology, has published a paper outlining the most conclusive evidence yet linking laughter and blood levels of immunoglobulin A. (This helps people fight illness by marking invading bacteria and viruses for destruction by white blood cells.) Melancholy people had higher levels of cortisones, which are associated with stress and can damage people's ability to fight disease. Only now is the role of their uplifting counterparts, the cytokines, beginning to be understood.

God has given us a prescription for joy. All we have to do is fill the prescription.[79]

MARILYN MEBERG

WEEKEND

YOUR PRAISE IS BEAUTIFUL

You who are godly, sing with joy to the LORD.
It is right for honest people to praise him....
He heals those who have broken hearts.
He takes care of their wounds.

PSALM 33:1; 147:3 NIRV

Our longing to see the face of God is a longing, whether we know it or not, to see our sins exposed and to be cleansed. This is what brides-in-waiting do: "'His bride has made herself ready. Fine linen, bright and clean, was given her to wear,' (Fine linen stands for the righteous acts of the saints.)" (Revelation 19:7–8). Your wedding gift to your Savior is your earthly obedience, the evidence of your love. Dressed in righteousness, you will see the face of God! Make your praise beautiful today—he thinks it's lovely, and he takes great joy in it!

JONI EARECKSON TADA

Dear Lord, thank you for exposing my sin and
cleansing me. The prayer of my heart today is the words
of Psalm 42: "As the deer pants for streams of water, so my
soul pants for you, O God. My soul thirsts for God, for the
living God. When can I go and meet with God?" Amen. [80]

MONDAY

JESUS RESTORES DIGNITY

If we walk in the light, as he is in the light,
we have fellowship with one another, and the
blood of Jesus, his Son, purifies us from all sin.

1 JOHN 1:7

I have a friend who is a missionary on the border between Thailand and Cambodia. One of his concerns is for people who are suffering from leprosy. He and his colleagues began to spend time with those men and women, doing what they could to aid them physically and spiritually. Eventually a church was born, right in the middle of a leper camp. A man who had been among the first to make a commitment to following Christ said, "Now I can look you in the face. I was too ashamed before because of my disfigurement, but now that I know how much Jesus loves me, I think that I can hold my head up high."

That is how it is supposed to be for us all. Jesus has restored our dignity. We all struggle with our humanity, but cleansing is not found in the shadows; it is found in the burning light.[81] And that is cause for rejoicing!

SHEILA WALSH

TUESDAY

❋

BE A JOY GERM

Encourage one another and build each other up,
just as in fact you are doing.

1 THESSALONIANS 5:11

Someone you know is crossing a desert in her life and could use a drink of cold water. Will you be the one to bring it to her? Take up your pen! In the deserts of life, hearts shrivel up. We can't let others dehydrate from neglect.

Why not clear out a drawer in your kitchen and fill it with stationery, pens, and fun stickers? In between clean-up jobs or while you're watching the potatoes bake, you can jot a little love letter to someone. Get your kids into the act! Teach them early to think of the needs of others and reach out in a tangible way. A few words is all it takes. If you know someone who is going through a long-term sorrow, pre-address and stamp some envelopes so it's easy to jot a thought and drop it in the mailbox once or twice a month.

Be a "joy germ" and find your own unique way to share a word of encouragement today. Someone you know needs it![82]

BARBARA JOHNSON

WEDNESDAY

❋

SONGS OF PRAISE

The LORD is my strength and my song;
  he has become my salvation.
He is my God, and I will praise him,
  my father's God, and I will exalt him.

EXODUS 15:2

The entire chapter of Exodus 15 is a song of joy and praise! The Lord had just opened a path through the Red Sea, and you can imagine the Israelites' amazement when they saw the water parted like giant glass skyscrapers. But a few verses later, their joy turned sour. As soon as they ran into trouble, the songs quickly faded. The irony is, they grumbled about water! Hadn't they just watched God part a whole sea of it?

Our own songs of praise fade all too quickly when we forget how God protects and provides for us. We need to take the advice God gave the Israelites in Deuteronomy 4:9: "Only be careful and watch yourselves closely so that you do not forget the things your eyes have seen."

The next time you're tempted to grumble or complain, think of your favorite praise song and then sing it. It will be God's way of helping you not to forget his protection and provision in your life.[83]

JONI EARECKON TADA

THURSDAY

❁

TRUE GENEROSITY

You will be made rich in every way so that you can be generous on every occasion, and through us your generosity will result in thanksgiving to God.

2 CORINTHIANS 9:11

Are you a truly generous person? Do you give of yourself, as well as of your resources? Have you ever given your time and strength at the bedside of a sick friend? Have you prayed long and tenaciously for another person?

We all know that giving of ourselves brings bounteous blessings to others and increases our joy, as well. But sometimes we cry out that we have no more to give, that we have exceeded the limits allowed.

What happens, though, when God makes it clear we are to give beyond what we think we are able? Then, giving becomes an act of faith—and another way to experience God. As we look to him for the provision to give to others, we discover a special closeness to God. And we understand more what it cost him to be generous toward us.[84]

JANET KOBOBEL GRANT

FRIDAY

PUT AWAY YOUR COUPONS

God's divine power has given us everything we need for life and godliness through our knowledge of him who called us by his own glory and goodness.

2 PETER 1:3

Coupons save time and money. They provide immediate results and less expensive ways to have what we want or need. That's nice. But you know what? In God's economy, there are no coupons or discounts. And do you know why? Because we don't need them! Discounts are unnecessary.

Imagine! He has given us everything we need.

Unfortunately, most of us go through life feeling as if we're long on need and short on resources. So we look for coupons. We present various offerings to the Lord as if he were some grocery-store clerk, making promises and hoping God will redeem them. In the process, we miss the essence of what Peter taught. He assures us that, in Christ, and through his goodness, you and I have everything we need for life. When Christ redeemed us, he made coupon redemption superfluous.

God has promised his fullness. No half remedies. No special deals. So take joy in his provision—and put away your coupons.[85]

LUCI SWINDOLL

WEEKEND

❋

ORDINARY GIRL,
EXTRAORDINARY GOD

*[I pray] that the communication of thy faith
may become effectual by the acknowledging of
every good thing which is in you in Christ Jesus.*

PHILEMON 6 KJV

I sang at a fundraising dinner in Chicago. At the end, a lady walked up to me. "Kathy, that song, 'My Life Is in Your Hands,' it absolutely broke my heart tonight. I have a husband in prison…" Incredibly, the woman was the wife of a prisoner, and she ended up calling him as a result of the words of my song. I understand they are back together again.

Was it anything I did? I believe not. Yes, I sang a song that stirred two hearts in such a way that they moved toward each other. But the truth is that I am an ordinary girl who happens to serve an extraordinary God. I need only attest to his mercy in my life, and he will do the rest.

Say yes to God. Give him permission to use you. Make yourself available to him, and watch miracles unfold before your eyes.[86]

KATHY TROCCOLI

*Heavenly Father, I say yes to you and give you permission
to use me to reach others. Amen.*

Monday

The Fruit of Joy

The fruit the Holy Spirit produces is love, joy and peace. It is being patient, kind and good. It is being faithful and gentle and having control of oneself. There is no law against things of that kind.

GALATIANS 5:22–23 NIRV

The apostle Paul wrote that joy is a fruit of lives that are lived in and with the Spirit of God. But what does that mean? It means that joy is not something you can buy or chase. You can't get it from a book or a conference. You can't absorb it by hanging out with people who seem to have it.

You can spend your life trying to eliminate all pain and stress from your world in the vain hope that joy will take its place. It won't. You can beg for it, pray for it, or bargain for it, to no avail. Because joy comes only when you live in relationship with the source of joy. It is the fruit of our relationship with him.

If God is the source of our joy, the size of the joy he wants to grow in us is "inexpressible and glorious" (1 Peter 1:8). Watch out for the amazing harvest![87]

SHEILA WALSH

TUESDAY

PRAYERS OF PRAISE

God raised us up with Christ and seated us with him in the heavenly realms in Christ Jesus, in order that in the coming ages he might show the incomparable riches of his grace, expressed in his kindness to us in Christ Jesus.

EPHESIANS 2:6—7

In your mind's eye, where is your place before God when you pray? Do you see yourself coming to him with cap in hand to beg? Do you feel a little out of place in the divine throne room? Perhaps you picture yourself at a distance from God—timid, shy, and imploring the Lord to do something.

There may be times when it's appropriate to go to God as a beggar or seriously mourn over some terrible transgression. But even in those times of sorrow, God wants you to understand your glorious position in prayer. For when you come before God to praise and intercede, it is your privilege and pleasure to join with Christ where he is seated at God's right hand. In that sacred spot, even a beggar becomes a child of the king.

Whey you pray, remember that even your most feeble and faint prayer shakes the hearts of the people for whom you intercede. It's a privilege. It's a responsibility. It's a joy![88]

JONI EARECKSON TADA

WEDNESDAY

❁

PLAYTIME

May the righteous be glad
and rejoice before God;
may they be happy and joyful.

PSALM 68:3

They say three kinds of people populate the world: Those who can count and those who can't. As you can see, I'm in the latter category. Despite my math deficiency, uncertainty, and puzzlement, there's one problem I don't have. I'm not like certain pious Christians who suffer from the haunting fear that someone, somewhere, may be happy.

We have to be on the lookout for fun, whether it be in simple things like funny signs ("Our fish are so fresh you want to smack 'em!"); funny names (if Fanny Brice had married Vic Tanny); or funny bumper stickers ("Forget about world peace. Visualize using your turn signal.")

Find out what brings you joy. Have fun in a myriad of ways. Don't put it off until you finish your chores; instead, make tedious tasks a game. Compete with yourself. Reward yourself. Make work, play. Be curious about everything and everyone. You'll get tickled in the process![89]

BARBARA JOHNSON

THURSDAY

❋

FROSTY BLESSING

It was good for me to be afflicted
so that I might learn your decrees.

PSALM 119:71

The crocuses in my backyard are fragrant and beautiful, even in the dry, warm climate of Southern California. I don't know how to account for such a profusion of flowers except to say that we had a couple weeks of hard frost back in January. I'm only an amateur gardener, but I'm convinced the freezing cold forced an unusual degree of beauty out of my crocuses.

A theologian who also knew something about gardening once said, "The nipping frosts of trial and affliction are oft times needed if God's trees are to grow. They need the cold to revive the bud." What is true for crocuses is also true for people.

Do you feel the nipping frost of loneliness? Are you experiencing the biting cold of persecution? For you, it could be the icy sting of rejection or the numbing chill of heartache. Just as flower bulbs need the nipping frost to revive and blossom, in your life, patience can flower out of failure, and self-control or kindness can bud out of brokenness.[90]

JONI EARECKSON TADA

FRIDAY

COUNTING THE COST

Jesus said, "Anyone who does not take his cross and follow me is not worthy of me. Whoever finds his life will lose it, and whoever loses his life for my sake will find it."

MATTHEW 10:38–39

With eyes full of love and compassion, Jesus extends his hand and offers us life abundant and joyful, here and for eternity. "But how much will it cost?" you ask. The answer is short, simple, and painful. "It will cost you everything," the Lord replies.

Ouch. That's what the rich young ruler must have said when he asked Jesus how he could have eternal life. The Lord commanded the young man to sell everything he had, give the money to the poor, and follow him as his Lord. The man couldn't bear the cost, and he walked away the loser.

What was true for the rich young ruler is still true for us. God seems to always be pointing to one more area of our lives that needs to come under his domain. "Ouch," we reply, "Lord, haven't you asked enough of me?" You can be sure that at whatever point you resist, God will persevere.[91]

JONI EARECKSON TADA

WEEKEND

❋

NEVER MORE THAN WE CAN BEAR

He will not let you be tempted beyond what
you can bear. . . . He will also provide a way out
so that you can stand up under it.

1 CORINTHIANS 10:13

God, in his mercy, out of a desire for a real relationship
with us, will continue to allow us to fall flat on our
faces until all we want is him. He is so committed to our spiritual health and growth that he will do whatever it takes to
free us from our selfish nature. But this is no mindless, bar-
baric endurance test. He knows us well and loves us lavishly.

God's purposes are for our good, never for our destruction. We have the comfort of knowing that God, who created
us, who knew us before we were born, and who perfectly
knows us now, has promised us that he will not permit us to
be given more than we can bear.[92]

SHEILA WALSH

Heavenly Father, you are good, and you are love.
Because of that, I can trust you with my whole heart.
Thank you for not allowing more to come into my life
than I can stand, for showing me the way out,
and for giving me joy throughout the journey. Amen.

MONDAY

❋

GOD'S ENDLESS LOVE

The LORD is gracious and compassionate,
  slow to anger and rich in love.

PSALM 145:8

Late one afternoon when I was ten, Papa read to me from the Bible. When he finished reading, I asked him a question about God's love: "Papa, will God ever stop loving me?"

Papa smiled, and from his Bible he read to me from Romans, where God promises us he will love us forever, without condition. "Who shall separate us from the love of Christ? Shall trouble or hardship or persecution or famine or nakedness or danger or sword?...No, in all these things we are more than conquerors through him who loved us." (Romans 8:35, 37).

When my grandfather finished reading, he wiped his sky-blue eyes with a hankerchief, and said: "'Nisey, God will always love you, no matter what. 'God is love.'"

My grandfather spent most of his life telling people that God loved them and that God would never stop loving them. He knew how desperately humanity wanted and needed love. We are a world starved for affection, love, and acceptance—a society in need of a hug, a warm hand, a human touch. Take joy in showing someone God's love today.[93]

DENISE GEORGE

TUESDAY

AT THE FOOT OF MOUNT ZION

May the LORD bless you from Zion
all the days of your life.

PSALM 128:5

My spirit soars when I look up at the snow-capped Sierras. Even though they're grand and glacier-scarred, their beauty makes them approachable. I don't feel that way about the volcano at the northern edge of the same range. There's nothing approachable about Mount Saint Helens.

Hebrews 12 reads like a topography of mountains. Mount Sinai burns with fire and is surrounded by darkness and lightning. Even Moses was afraid of it. But then there's Mount Zion, a place of angelic joy and happy assembly. Two mountains. Two views of life. One depicts a God of gloom and doom. The other represents a God of joy and forgiveness. How often we find ourselves living in the frightening shadows of Mount Sinai, confronted by our inability to live up to the demands of a holy God, consumed by guilt, and backsliding in despair.

Don't pitch your tent at the foot of that fearful mountain. Brush up on your topography and walk in the direction of Mount Zion today.[94]

JONI EARECKSON TADA

WEDNESDAY

❖

STOP COMPARING

We do not dare to classify or compare
ourselves with some who commend themselves.
When they measure themselves by themselves and
compare themselves with themselves, they are not wise.

2 CORINTHIANS 10:12

When Scripture teaches that it is not wise to measure or compare ourselves with others, I think we should pay attention. When we compare, we almost always come up short. Or, perhaps worse, we decide we're better than someone else. Either way, it causes stress in our lives.

If you're not happy with who you are, you'll spend precious energy trying to be somebody you're not, and it will wear you out. Think for a moment. Is there anybody in your life to whom you're comparing yourself? Well, may I say with all the love in the world: *Quit it!* That business of comparing is going to make you sick and unproductive, if it hasn't already. You are you. God made you, you. And you are exactly who he wants you to be. Don't be somebody's clone. That person you're trying to be may very well be trying to be you. Where's the joy in that? Let's just all relax and be ourselves. It's so much easier and a lot more fun.[95]

LUCI SWINDOLL

THURSDAY

❋

HE WILL TAKE YOU THERE

They that wait upon the LORD shall renew their strength;
they shall mount up with wings as eagles; they shall run,
and not be weary; and they shall walk, and not faint.

ISAIAH 40:31 KJV

O ften in my journey up the mountains and through the
valleys, I want to set up camp. Sometimes it's because
of brokenness and weariness; I feel I can't possibly go on, or
I don't want to go on, so I stop walking. I am learning that the
only time I can stop walking is when I am in a holy resting
place, a place in which I acknowledge my weariness and
frailty, and Jesus is carrying me or I am sleeping in his arms.
Knowing I'm yielding to his will and voice, knowing I can't
go places where the Holy Spirit has to go, I pray and lay my
life in God's hands.

Let the Lord have his complete way with you. He loves
you so much and has far greater plans for you than you can
ever have for yourself. Allow God to move in you powerfully.
Yield to his voice—calling deeper—higher still. He will take
you there,[96] to a place of joy and contentment.

KATHY TROCCOLI

FRIDAY

※

FLINGING JOY

As we have opportunity, let us do good to all people,
especially to those who belong to the family of believers.

GALATIANS 6:10

As I travel across the country to various speaking engage-
ments, I meet lots of hurting people. Pain is a normal
part of life. That's why I think to myself: *Why not take as much joy*
as possible along the way so when pain comes, we assimilate it better?

Every day I take joy—how? First, I refuse to accept the
line that I have to feel miserable about the baggage and the
sickness that trails me no matter how I try to hide or outwit
it. Second, I choose to do zany, kooky, funny things to make
myself and others laugh.

I fling joy—beyond my next-door neighbor's fence, clear
across town, and into the universe. Then it curves right back
to me. Sometimes with a whack on the head when I need it.
Sometimes with a thwack into my heart. Sometimes it lands
with a crack at my feet. But it always comes back.[97]

BARBARA JOHNSON

WEEKEND

❖

SPONTANEOUS JOY

Jesus said, "Unless you change and become like little children, you will never enter the kingdom of heaven. Therefore, whoever humbles himself like this child is the greatest in the kingdom of heaven."

MATTHEW 18:3–4

The longer I live, the more I realize that the ability to find joy in life really is a tremendous strength. The people who can laugh are the strong ones. The people who can throw their heads back and delight in the joy of the moment are going to live a lot longer than those of us who are stressed and pushed and taking ourselves terribly seriously.

Children really are good at openhearted, spontaneous joy. They know it intuitively. That's why they use it lavishly in the present moment. They don't put it in a savings account for a rainy day. They don't put it on hold or put a lid on it. They spend it with abandon. They practice it at every small occasion. That's why they are such pros at getting it right![98]

CLAIRE CLONINGER

Heavenly Father, give me the heart of a child—open to the blessing of spontaneous joy. Teach me to recognize joy wherever I go, relishing each giggle and unexpected smile. Amen.

MONDAY

HE'S LOOKING AT YOU

Keep me as the apple of your eye;
hide me in the shadow of your wings

PSALM 17:8

"I volunteered to sing at the local nursing home this past Sunday," she began. "I wanted to bring a little joy to the residents who don't get out much.

"Well, six people showed up. Three ladies fell asleep. Another was off in a corner dancing to a tune different from the one I was singing. The loudest one sat right up front. Her hearing aid was turned up too high, and it was giving off high-pitched whining noises. Every time I began another song, she cried out at the top of her lungs, 'Oh, no, she's going to sing again!'"

Do you ever feel as if no one seems to notice or appreciate you? God sees your heart, and that's all he cares about. He doesn't miss a single moment of a life lived out for him. If everyone in your audience has dozed off or danced off to another tune, you might want to check again. There, in the corner, is God, watching and listening and appreciating you.⁹⁹

SHEILA WALSH

TUESDAY

❋

INNER JOY

My soul finds rest in God alone;
my salvation comes from him.

PSALM 62:1

Solitude can frighten us if we don't grasp its spiritual significance. But if we squarely face ourselves and offer up
the emptiness to God, our aloneness can forge a path to inner
joy. Teresa of Avila of ancient times advised, "Settle yourself in
solitude and you will come upon him in yourself." When
invited, God fills empty souls with himself, and in his presence
"is fullness of joy." With this joy, our solitude tastes sweet, for
we're passing time with the attentive lover of our souls.

Yet this joyful solitude may not arrive swiftly or easily. This
joy must be hoped for, prayed for, and allowed the luxury of
time to infuse the soul. It may require repeated ventures into
aloneness before it manifests itself. God does not arrive and
perform on demand. He waits until our hearts are ready. But
when we do achieve joyful solitude, it is just what we need to
carry us through the busy and uncertain days ahead.[100]

JUDITH COUCHMAN

WEDNESDAY

❋

GRACIOUS WORDS AND ACTS

The LORD shows unfailing kindness to his anointed,
to David and his descendants forever.

PSALM 18:50

A ren't you glad God is sweet to us, that he goes the extra
mile to be kind even when we are undeserving? His
constancy should cause us to want to express our love and
appreciation to others in gracious words and acts every day.
Loneliness and isolation abound in the world, right in our
neighborhoods, perhaps in our own homes. We all carry
secrets—painful secrets that make us feel scared, alone, and
sometimes alienated. If we knew how many secret feelings of
pain resided in our own household, we would be amazed.

Don't misunderstand. I don't believe we can humanly
alleviate loneliness nor crank out friendliness, kindness, or
sweetness day after day—unless it comes through the power
of God's indwelling Spirit. A personal relationship with God,
through faith in his Son, Jesus Christ, puts us in touch with the
supernatural power to greet people on the freeway with a
smile instead of a frown.[101]

LUCI SWINDOLL

THURSDAY

✻

REJOICE IN THE MOMENT

Be very careful how you live. Do not live like people
who aren't wise. Live like people who are wise.
Make the most of every opportunity.

EPHESIANS 5:15–16 NIRV

Look at the life you hold in your own two hands. Is it tattered and shabby? Think about it. Might it bring opportunities for growth and gladness? What is going to be important one hundred years from now that doesn't seem important now? What seems important now that will not be important a century from now?

In moments that appear unredeemable, watch and wait. Recognize the precious things. Refuse to trash anything! Ask God to help you see things from his perspective. Take one step after another. Before long, you may notice surprising signs of hope in your own backyard.

Trial and triumph are what God uses to scribble all over the pages of our lives. They are signs that he is using us, loving us, shaping us to his image, enjoying our companionship, delivering us from evil, and writing eternity into our hearts. Be happy through everything, because today is the only thing you can be sure of. Enjoy the moment you hold in your hands.[102]

BARBARA JOHNSON

FRIDAY

SHOCKING-PINK JOY

Your troubles have come in order to prove that
your faith is real. It is worth more than gold. Gold can
pass away even though fire has made it pure. Your faith
is meant to bring praise, honor and glory to God.

1 PETER 1:7 NIRV

Have you ever noticed that our lives are made up of laughter and tears, dirges and dances, jubilations and consternations, hallelujahs and woes? We have good days, great days, and way-down-deep-in-the-pit days. For each of us, our days are unpredictable, and we tip the scales from preposterous to precious. Life is a gift bulging with mystery, intrigue, comedy, tragedy—and purpose.

When we realize that our days here matter, that our pain has significance, and that our choices are meaningful, we can walk through the darkest of times with hope in our hearts.

I find that my joy is enlarged by understanding that, as a child of God, even my pain has purpose. That realization doesn't eliminate my pain, but it makes it more manageable, allowing me other emotions in the mist of calamity, including shocking-pink joy.[103]

PATSY CLAIRMONT

WEEKEND

✦

STEP INTO THE LIGHT

You, O LORD, keep my lamp burning;
my God turns my darkness into light.

PSALM 18:28

C.S. Lewis describes surrendering ourselves to God as the difference between looking *along* a beam of light and looking into a beam of light. In a book of essays entitled *God in the Dock*, he describes this experience as it happened to him while sitting in a tool shed. He was watching a shaft of sunlight pouring through a crack in the wood. It was the only thing that he could see—everything else was dark—until he stood up and looked through the beam. Then, everything was changed; he could not see the beam at all, and yet the scene outside the woodshed was illuminated.

We can choose to live in the darkness, observing life from the safety of the sidelines, or we can step into the light and be given a bigger vision.[104]

SHEILA WALSH

> *Heavenly Father, thank you that you have not left me to*
> *stumble around in the darkness alone, but you sent Jesus*
> *to be the light of my world. I surrender all to you. Amen.*

Monday

✦

Heavenly-Minded People

The mind set on the flesh is death,
but the mind set on the Spirit is life and peace.

ROMANS 8:6 NASB

C.S. Lewis said, "Aim at heaven, and you get earth thrown in. Aim at earth and you get neither." What happens when your heart and mind are set on things above?

Unlike the person whose mind is on earthly things, you begin to see yourself as a sojourner, a pilgrim on earth. You begin to appreciate your citizenship in heaven. You also begin to eagerly await the Lord's return, and you anticipate the joy of having him transform your body into one like his.

Those whose destiny is destruction may say that being so heavenly minded makes you no earthly good. Not so! Those whose minds are on heaven do the earth a world of good.

When you realize that your citizenship is in heaven, you begin acting as a responsible citizen should. You begin to invest wisely in relationships. Your conversations, goals, and motives become more pure and honest, and all of this serves you well, not only in heaven but also here on earth. Heavenly-minded people are for the earth's highest good.[105]

JONI EARECKSON TADA

TUESDAY

GOD IN OUR CIRCUMSTANCE

We also rejoice in our sufferings, because we know that suffering produces perseverance; perseverance, character; and character, hope. And hope does not disappoint us, because God has poured out his love into our hearts by the Holy Spirit, whom he has given us.

ROMANS 5:3–5

I would like God to involve himself in my circumstances according to my timing and my agenda. I forget how holy and perfect his ways, his timing, and his agenda really are. Yet, over and over I see that when I wait, letting him be God, then he *is* God.

The circumstances of life can embitter any of us at any time. But if we allow it, God's grace and love can empower us and help us move through these times victoriously. As Oswald Chambers said, "It is not our circumstance, but God in our circumstance."

More and more, I'm learning to embrace what life has to offer, to soak the poison out of it by taking in God's love in a way that helps me do, act, and say exactly what is in *his* heart to do, act, and say. And I only become a better woman for it. My heart continues to grow wider so that more of Jesus can dwell in me.[106] Consequently, my joy becomes more full.

KATHY TROCCOLI

WEDNESDAY

❁

GOD'S LOVE SONG FOR YOU

The LORD will take delight in you,
and in his love he will give you new life.
He will sing and be joyful over you.

ZEPHANIAH 3:17 GNT

When my heart is restless and my soul is downcast, I often surround myself with the calming strains of a favorite hymn. Sometimes when I want to express sheer praise, I'll pick a happy psalm and just put it to any old tune that comes to mind. I sing to myself. I sing to God. But I'm astonished to think that God sings to me.

When God sings, do you think he sings all four parts at once? Maybe his music, so celestial and heavenly, resounds like a great choir. No doubt he has invented chords and dischords, major and minor keys that our ears have never heard. And I'm touched that he rejoices over you and me with an actual melody. What's more, he quiets us with his loving song.

I have often thought of this when a beautiful hymn keeps rolling over and over in my mind. I'm convinced that God is rejoicing over me with singing, hallelujah, and all I need to do is listen and be inspired.[107]

JONI EAREKCSON TADA

THURSDAY

❋

FLYING COLORS

Just as you received Christ Jesus as Lord,
continue to live in him, rooted and built up in him,
strengthened in the faith as you were taught,
and overflowing with thankfulness.

COLOSSIANS 2:6–7

Everybody experiences difficult situations in life. Everybody. Things that make us want to scream out or give up. Deprivations. Sacrifices. Losses. Misunderstandings. But isn't there some way for the Christian to respond without getting mad at God? Otherwise, what's the good of our faith? There has to be some key to being joyful in the midst of discouraging circumstances and crabby people. What is it?

It's taking God at his Word. It's believing he will do what he says, no matter how things look or how we feel. Nobody said it would be easy. If you find any Scripture that even hints that life will be easy, call me collect. Please. But I can tell you now… it ain't in there! However, trusting God with everything we have and everything we are, with every problem that is ours, every loss we endure, every battle we face, every person who disappoints us—with thanksgiving—gives us the grace to come through it with flying colors.[108]

LUCI SWINDOLL

FRIDAY

A THANK-YOU LETTER

I thank my God every time I remember you....
It is right for me to feel this way about all of you.
I love you with all my heart.

PHILIPPIANS 1:3, 7 NIRV

Paul's letter to the Philippians is different from his others. Philippians is not a theology lesson, or a manual on how to solve problems. Philippians is a thank-you letter, and because of that, Paul doesn't watch his words but writes an endless stream of joyful remembrances and encouragements. You can tell that he had fun with his pen and paper.

How poignantly Paul wrote his thank-you letter from a dark, stinking prison cell. That he can say, "be anxious about nothing," and, "I've learned to be content," while in bruising chains makes the book of Philippians all the more joyful.

You may not be in an actual prison, but like the apostle, you may feel chained to a few unpleasant circumstances. If so, are you still able to write a thank-you letter to God? If you need help composing your words, take time to flip open to the book of Philippians and peruse the finest thank-you letter ever written.[109]

JONI EARECKSON TADA

WEEKEND

✦

CRY OUT TO HIM

The eyes of the LORD are on the righteous
and his ears are attentive to their cry.

PSALM 34:15

For any number of reasons, many of us live on the edge of a volcano. So I say…let's let our anger out; let's cry out our hurt and pain and fear until we have no tears left. Anger needs to be expressed, and it is much better for us to cry it out to God than to machine-gun our friends with it.

If the whole purpose of our lives on this earth is to glorify God and enjoy him forever, then I believe he is the one to whom we can bring the emotions that tear at our hearts. As we bare our souls before him, he will trade our unbearable burdens for a load that we can carry.

SHEILA WALSH

Father God, hear my prayer. I bring my fear to you.
I bring my rage to you. I bring the broken pieces of
my life. Teach me to live lightly, casting my cares on you.
Thank you that I can bury my face in you. Amen.[110]

MONDAY

KNEE-DEEP IN PENGUINS

Sing for joy to God our strength.

PSALM 81:1

Along with three friends, I flew to Chile for what proved to be a fantastic trip. I was utterly delighted as our bus made its way down to the coastal penguin rookery.

As we exited the bus, we stood literally knee-deep in penguins. Some awkwardly headed for the ocean where they fell in, while others milled about. One particularly friendly penguin turned to a woman and began an energetic effort to loosen her shoelaces. When the shoelaces would not yield, the penguin pummeled the woman's leg with a succession of flipper slaps that sent us all into hysterics.

To my knowledge, penguins don't serve any useful purpose in life other than to give pleasure to people like me. Perhaps God put together some things for no other reason than that we might "sing for joy at the works of his hands." From the grandeur of snow-capped peaks to the awkward land inefficiency of penguins, what fun it is simply to "sing for joy" about his creation.[111]

MARILYN MEBERG

TUESDAY

✦

THE GIFT OF FRIENDSHIP

Jesus said, "I no longer call you servants,
because a servant does not know his master's business.
Instead, I have called you friends, for everything that
I learned from my Father I have made known to you."

JOHN 15:15

Jesus Christ created a model of love, as he did of friendship: Along with the reassuring "I have loved you even as the Father has loved me...I have told you this so that your joy may be full," we hear from his heart the welcoming words, "I have called you friend." Mind-boggling!

When Jesus talked to his disciples, he didn't give long discourses on friendship. He demonstrated friendship by being available, compassionate, self-sacrificing, and tender. His chosen friends responded! Yes, he called them to accountability; he rebuked them when they were wrong. But when he was finished, they still felt cherished by him. What a picture!—another of his gifts to us—to be treasured, to be emulated—to be enjoyed.

We must simply set out to be the friend Christ modeled—anticipating the needs of others, wearing ourselves out at giving. The rewards are infinite and joyous![112]

JOY BUCHANAN

WEDNESDAY

❋

HE DELIGHTS IN YOU

The LORD will take delight in you....
As a bridegroom rejoices over his bride,
so will your God rejoice over you.

ISAIAH 62:4–5

I asked my husband, Ken, on our tenth wedding anniversary, "What were you thinking on the day we married?" His answer delighted me. He said, "I woke up so early that morning, excited that I would soon see you in your wedding gown. And even though I knew there would be hundreds of people in the church, I knew my eyes would be for you, only. In fact, I'll never forget that wonderful feeling when I saw you wheeling down the aisle in your chair, you looked so beautiful."

Hearing those words gave me so much pleasure. And just think. This is the way God feels toward us. We give him great joy. He finds pleasure and satisfaction in our worship and praise. And our obedience brings a smile to his face.

Love him today with all your heart. After all, every day his heart is full of love for you.[113]

JONI EARECKSON TADA

WEEKEND

✿

NEVER FEAR, GOD IS NEAR

Do not fear, for I am with you;
  do not be dismayed, for I am your God.
I will strengthen you and help you;
  I will uphold you with my righteous right hand.

ISAIAH 41:10

As he lay in a Roman cell awaiting execution, Paul wrote to his friends in Philippi: "Rejoice in the Lord always. I will say it again: Rejoice! Let your gentleness be evident to all. The Lord is near. Do not be anxious about anything" (Philippians 4:4–6). Paul was in the clutches of Nero, an evil, brutish emperor who delighted in the suffering of others. History tells us Nero would hold feasts on the palace grounds and illuminate the proceedings with the burning bodies of Christians. Yet Paul was not afraid. He had been through the fires of suffering, and his sights were set on a land Nero could not touch.

First John 4:18 says that "perfect love drives out fear." God will do what it takes until that love is perfected in us. And as we listen, he will show us the next step in our ministry—the work he has appointed us to do—whether it is quietly singing songs to young lambs or publicly proclaiming his grace.[114]

SHEILA WALSH

MONDAY

✦

THE LORD OF JOY

The joy of the LORD makes you strong.

NEHEMIAH 8:10 NIRV

Stop and muse for a moment on the joy of the Lord. Consider his gift of the Spirit-inspired fruit of joy. His oft-repeated command was, "Rejoice!" Fullness of joy is to be found in him. For the joy that was set before him, Jesus endured his cross. If you're looking for joy, it can only be found in one place, or, that is, one Person—the Lord of Joy.

Now place yourself back in time. Jesus laughs as he holds a neighbor's newborn baby. He smiles while bouncing a three-year-old child on his knee. He tousles the hair of a rowdy little boy. Picture his joy to watch a puppy at play, to hear a funny story, to taste a hot and savory stew. Feel his joy when the disciples listened and obeyed. Think of the joy that seized him at the sight of a glorious sunset knowing he created it. And finally, Jesus' joy at seeing his Father's dream fulfilled.

Meditate on God's smile, and his joy will be yours.[115]

JONI EARECKSON TADA

WEEKEND

❋

BE A BLESSING

God said, "I will surely bless you and make
your descendants as numerous as the stars in the sky
and as the sand on the seashore.... Through your
offspring all nations on earth will be blessed,
because you have obeyed me."

GENESIS 22:17—18

Would you like to have assurance that you are enjoying the Lord's favor? Ask yourself these questions:

Is the joy of your relationship with Jesus overflowing to those around you? Is their walk with him different because of you? Is their prayer life growing because of you? Has their witness gone up a notch because something about you has rubbed off on them? If so, rest assured. God's blessing is on you.

To be blessed by God means being deeper, higher, and farther into his heart. Being blessed means *feeling* his favor, his pleasure, and his delight. It means understanding him in his ways. What a joyful gift to pass on to others.[116]

JONI EARECKSON TADA

Lord, the best blessing you can ever bestow on me is Jesus.
Thank you for sending him to die for me on the cross.
Help me to get to know his heart and understand his ways.
In turn I'll pass on the blessing that results to others. Amen.

MONDAY

A DAILY DOSE OF JOY

I thank my God every time I remember you.
In all my prayers for all of you, I always pray with joy.

PHILIPPIANS 1:3–4

I love greeting cards—the way they make me feel when I receive them and when I give them. We exchange greetings at the traditional times and then there are those wonderful "for nothing" times. Sometimes tender, sometimes funny, these sweet gifts show up in a mailbox or on a windshield, in a book or a suitcase.

I appreciate the opportunity to express my feelings for someone in a way that uniquely fits that person or the situation in that person's life. However long or short—writing our feelings down and sending them is always worth the time and energy. It's amazing what often transpires. Smiles, tears, hugs, encouragement, healing. Cold walls melt, hard days take an easier turn, and bitterness gives way to forgiveness. The saying that life is far too short and unpredictable is absolutely true. I try not to let a day go by without saying what needs to be said—or even what needs to be said again.[117] It guarantees a daily dose of joy.

KATHY TROCCOLI

TUESDAY

WHAT KEEPS YOU FROM SOARING?

If any of you need wisdom, ask God for it.
He will give it to you.

JAMES 1:5 NIRV

I was flying from Minneapolis to California, or so I thought, when the pilot announced that we were returning to our port of departure. *Whatever for?* we all wondered, groaning and complaining. The pilot explained that the aircraft couldn't get enough altitude to clear the Rocky Mountains near Denver. Despite our mutterings, we turned around and headed back.

Once on the ground, it wasn't long before the airplane mechanics found the problem. One of them had left a vacuum hose in the door, preventing the seal from being tight enough to allow the cabin to be pressurized and thus enable the plane to clear the Rockies. A simple error by a careless mechanic drained the airplane's power to soar.

What's the personal vacuum hose that keeps you from soaring? Pray for illumination. Do whatever is necessary to remove the hoses that drain your energy and joy. Don't give up and take the bus. It's better to fly.[118]

BARBARA JOHNSON

WEDNESDAY

❋

CHOOSING COURAGEOUSLY

God says,
"Be still, and know that I am God."

PSALM 46:10

It's easy to be fooled into thinking that our needs can be met in worldly pursuits or in people. But careers invariably come to an end. People consistently fail to meet our expectations. Dreams regularly fade away in the daylight.

If we try to find our identity in, or fix our vision on, these things rather than on Christ, our hearts remain restless, our arms vacant, our thoughts unfocused.

Nevertheless, we can courageously choose—over and over again—to open our hearts to the Word of God. We can stretch out our empty arms to embrace our loving Redeemer. We can sit down and surrender our distracting thoughts to receive the quiet stillness of the Holy Spirit's presence.

For the hungry, the empty, and the distracted, the message of Christ is the same. Jesus speaks of pardon and forgiveness, of joy and peace, given freely to all who look to him alone to satisfy their needs.[119]

DEBRA EVANS

WEEKEND

❋

PAY ATTENTION
IN THE DARKNESS

Whether you turn to the right or to the left,
your ears will hear a voice behind you, saying,
"This is the way; walk in it."

ISAIAH 30:21

In *Healing the Shame That Binds You*, John Bradshaw tells of a man who was sentenced to die and placed in a dark cave. He was told that there was a way out, and if he could find it within thirty days, he would be free. High above him, there was a small hole through which food was lowered to him. The man spent every waking moment trying to build a pile of stones high enough to climb to the top, to that tiny shaft of light, but by the time he got close to the hole, he was so exhausted from his efforts that he fell to his death.

If the prisoner had only known that one of the stones in the side of the cave had been pushed away, he could have escaped. None of us would seek pain, but when you find yourself in a bleak place, pay attention to what God would say to you in the darkness.[120] Allow his joy to be your strength.

SHEILA WALSH

MONDAY

THE BUTTERFLY OF HAPPINESS

*We are full of joy because we expect to share in
God's glory. And that's not all. We are full of joy even
when we suffer. We know that our suffering gives us
the strength to go on. The strength to go on
produces character. Character produces hope.*

ROMANS 5:2–4 NIRV

Some people are never going to be happy. Life, to them, seems
to be a never-ending drudgery of the same, sad routine.

Are you this way? Does happiness, like a butterfly, almost
flutter within reach, but just when you think you have grasped
it…it's gone? Or perhaps you feel your marriage is okay, and your
job is acceptable. Yet you feel as though something's missing.

Well, life is hard. Unhappiness seems to be here to stay.
But it doesn't have to be this way, because the answer is not to
get rid of unhappiness, but to find a new definition for it.

My friend Elisabeth Elliot has suggested that we redefine
happiness as duty and honor, sacrifice and faithfulness, commitment and service. Happiness is fleeting and elusive, but joy
is an overflow of the perseverance and hope that comes from
demonstrating faithful sacrifice and committed service.[121]

JONI EARECKSON TADA

WEEKEND

✳

THE CELEBRATION OF GOD

Glorify the LORD with me;
let us exalt his name together.

PSALM 34:3

The wisdom and doctrine of Scripture teach that the experience of celebrating God is the core of worship. It is the quintessence of praise and thanksgiving—the most perfect manifestation of a heart that gratefully fellowships with the One who provides life and all the gifts of living.

In fact, a grateful heart is not only the greatest virtue, it is the seedbed for all other virtues. When we are caught up into the celebration of God, there is neither room nor time for the invasion of negative living. As we rejoice before the Lord, as we serve him in the area of our calling, as we enter joyfully into our daily journey, as we give thanks to him for his kindness and faithfulness, we celebrate God.[122]

LUCI SWINDOLL

Heavenly Father, I come before you asking for a grateful
heart—a heart that is overflowing with thankfulness for
all of your blessings. Thank you for being more than
I could ever ask for or imagine. Amen.

MONDAY

SPIRITUAL INVENTORY

Be glad, O people of Zion,
rejoice in the LORD your God.
"I will repay you for the years the locusts have eaten."

JOEL 2:23, 25

I recently took inventory of my spiritual growth. As I marked off the milestones, I came across chunks of years that were spiritual wastelands.

In my early teens I turned down a summer missions trip because I didn't want to leave my boyfriend. Then came my accident. More years of spiritual dryness as I sneered at nurses and generally took my anger out on my family. But even after my accident, there were hidden sins that I covered up for months. A habit of prayer abandoned for almost a year. Bible reading ignored.

At the close of my spiritual inventory, I grieved to think what had been lost. But my grief lasted only a moment. God brought to mind the promise of Joel 2:25! The Lord promises that he will make good on the damage I've done. God vows that he will restore our loss. That's what restitution is all about.[123]

JONI EARECKSON TADA

TUESDAY

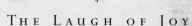

THE LAUGH OF JOY

Our mouths were filled with laughter,
*   our tongues with songs of joy.*
Then it was said among the nations,
*   "The LORD has done great things for them."*

PSALM 126:2

When doubts assail you, examine your heart. Is your doubt simply a mental questioning or testing? If so, don't berate yourself. Seek wisdom and continue to test all things. If your doubt arises from hardness of heart, repent and ask God for greater faith. It is only through your trust in him that your doubts will finally and fully be put to rest.

Consider Sarah, Abraham's wife. She laughed when God told her she would have a child in her old age. God gave her a son without regard to what she did. Her laugh of doubt was turned to a laugh of joy.

Even our lack of faith doesn't prevent God from keeping his promises and accomplishing what he plans. God is bigger than the weaknesses of men and women. The goal is to trust, and the power to trust is from the Lord.[124] Reach out to him, and trust him to change your laugh of doubt to a laugh of joy.

WOMEN OF FAITH STUDY BIBLE

WEDNESDAY

❋

TRIALS AND TEMPTATIONS

Blessed is the man who perseveres under trial,
because when he has stood the test, he will receive the
crown of life that God has promised to those who love him.

JAMES 1:12

Trials and temptations may sound like one and the same,
but they are not. A trial is a test that God puts before us
to prove our faith and produce perseverance. Trials are something we can face with joy.

There's nothing joyful about temptation. In fact, unlike
trials, God does not even place temptation in our path.
Temptations occur when we miss the God-given opportunity
to have our faith refined. At that point, a failed trial can turn
into a temptation when we are enticed to go our own way,
seek our own desires, or even grumble or complain.

James 1:16–17 says, "Don't be deceived, my dear brothers.
Every good and perfect gift is from above, coming down from
the Father of the heavenly lights." God never intends for trials
to turn into temptations; trials are his good and perfect gifts,
intended to refine our faith, develop perseverance, and make
us mature and complete.[125]

JONI EARECKSON TADA

THURSDAY

❖

FROM STRESSING TO BLESSING

Cast all your anxiety on him because he cares for you.

1 PETER 5:7

S tress is everywhere. People stress out because they know today is the tomorrow they worried about yesterday! Dieters know what stress is. Someone said, "I've been on a diet for two weeks, and all I've lost is fourteen days." That's self-imposed stress.

What happens when you think you are winning the rat race and along come faster rats? How do you deal with the stress? Stress may be a given factor, but your attitude can change the way it affects you.

Stress is nothing but psychological pollution. Flush stuff like that out of your system with a positive outlook. Keep mentally limber; accept what you can't change, and don't dwell on your own or others' shortcomings. Be an imp for a day or an hour, make a neighbor laugh, play a practical joke, delight yourself with a wacky surprise.

Don't waste today's time cluttering up tomorrow's opportunities with yesterday's troubles! God has promised to turn your "hours of stressing into showers of blessing."[126] That's something to rejoice about!

BARBARA JOHNSON

FRIDAY

SKIPPING AND JUMPING

Those who look at him are radiant;
their faces are never covered with shame.

PSALM 34:5

On a particularly damp and windy day, hundreds of calves were huddled outside, shoulder to hindquarter, tucked between the fence and the barn. They looked miserable. All except one calf. Although he, too, faced the same windy rain and was covered with the same mud, he chose a different shelter—an open field of muck! In the face of the wind, he skipped and jumped like a child. He was oblivious to the downpour. That calf literally looked happy.

Life is quite often like the farm scene of the calves, isn't it? We huddle with others of like misery, in the hopes that one day our lives will be happy again. Like the calf, however, David, the psalmist, chose to declare the joy of being a child of God. Are you gripped with a spirit of fear? Take each of your fears by the horn and lead it to the face of God. Let your fears see the light of eternal day and you, too, will skip, laugh, dance, and sing.[127]

JONI EARECKSON TADA

WEEKEND

❋

TO BE SURE

Jesus said, "Surely I am with you always, to the very end of the age."

I love to haunt old bookstores, antique shops, floral stores, and quaint little restaurants with a section of one-of-a-kind cards. I remember the day I picked up one that showed Winnie the Pooh and Piglet on the front walking hand in hand. Their conversation went like this:

"Pooh?" Piglet said.

"Yes, Piglet."

"Oh, nothing," Piglet said. "I just wanted to be sure of you."

The simplicity of that exchange between Pooh and Piglet mirrors an almost daily conversation between God and myself: "Jesus?" I say.

"Yes, Kathy."

"Oh, nothing," I say. "I just wanted to be sure of you."

My protector. My deliverer. My shelter. My Lord. If I can be sure of anything, I can be sure of him.[128]

KATHY TROCCOLI

Heavenly Father, thank you for being there for me, for never leaving me nor forsaking me. I am sure of this one thing—that you love me. My heart rejoices. Amen.

Monday

The Joy of Loving Others

*Since we are receiving a kingdom that cannot
be shaken, let us be thankful, and so worship
God acceptably with reverence and awe.*

HEBREWS 12:28

Many of us don't get the one thing we want most in our personal lives. Some of us dream of a spouse's love and don't have it, some desire children and don't have them. One of the greatest challenges in life is to accept the compensations God gives and, through Christ, live in faith and without envy, even when we don't get what we desire most deeply.

When we don't get what we deeply desire, it's easy to look only at what we don't have and ignore the good things we do have. Only Jesus Christ can help us rise above our needs and desires to find joy and purpose in loving others.

The "average" person today is called upon to balance a career, church, and community involvement with the changing needs of family and friends. Thankfully, on any given day, God promises to meet us where we are and never give us more than we can handle.[129]

DEBRA EVANS

TUESDAY

✦

A TRANSPARENT LIFE

Jesus said, "I have come so they can have life
I want them to have it in the fullest possible way."

JOHN 10:10 NIRV

I would imagine that in your circle of acquaintances, there are many who feel isolated, who long to live an honest, transparent life before others and before God. I am overwhelmed by the desire I see in people to live such a life.

If you have "been through the valley," perhaps God has anointed you to reach out and ask others around you to face the important questions of life: Do you know who you are? Do you long to say what you really think, rather than what you think you should say? Do you ever ask yourself who your real friends are, because you keep your life so guarded? Are you enjoying the awesome freedom that comes from realizing that Christ knows everything about you and loves you passionately? Are you really living, or are you just surviving?

I begin each day with a prayer of thanks that I am living in the midst of God's abundant, full life.[130]

SHEILA WALSH

WEDNESDAY

✦

FOUNTAIN OF JOY

On that day a fountain will be opened to the
house of David and the inhabitants of Jerusalem,
to cleanse them from sin and impurity.

ZECHARIAH 13:1

One hot summer day when I was a little girl, my mother took me to the park. As we strolled by a big fountain, I looked longingly as neighborhood children waded and splashed in the pool. I begged to join them and my mother did the most amazing thing—she let me.

She took off my shoes and socks, and I splashed in the fountain with the other children. My shorts and shirt were soaked, but there we were, a bunch of giggling boys and girls with arms widespread and faces uplifted, squealing as the water showered down on us. Our hearts were free. Exuberant. Full of life and in high spirits. A fountain is a place of joy.

God has opened up a fountain to you through the Lord Jesus. He invites you to come on in and enjoy his love. Don't stand on the edges of his joy. He has washed away your sin and you, like a child, can be free and full of life.[131]

JONI EARECKSON TADA

THURSDAY

❖

THE JOY OF GIVING

Jesus said, "Whoever believes in me, as the Scripture has said, streams of living water will flow from within him."

JOHN 7:38

You don't have to be wealthy to start giving to the poor. You don't have to be perfectly organized to start giving of your time. You don't have to have a beautiful home to invite other people in. You don't have to be especially gifted to start making a difference in this world.

If you don't have it all together, join the club. You want to minister or start on the road to success? Use what you have. Begin with the things in your hands. As you give out of your emptiness or loneliness, the gifts flow back your way. So don't wait another minute to give from what you have; begin today.

Don't wait to start smiling if you're feeling blue. The Lord gives us a face, but it's up to us to provide the expression. And once the joy of giving gets in your system, it's bound to break out on your face. [132]

BARBARA JOHNSON

FRIDAY

REAP SONGS OF JOY

Those who sow in tears
will reap with songs of joy.
He who goes out weeping,
carrying seed to sow,
will return with songs of joy,
carrying sheaves with him.

PSALM 126:5–6

When you sow in tears, what a marvelous and abundant return you will enjoy on your investment. *But, you may be thinking, when have I ever gone out weeping, carrying seed to sow?*

If you have ever reached through an invisible wall of pain to embrace God with willful thanks, you have sown in tears. If you've ever been rejected by a dear one and yet turned the other cheek in love, you have sown in tears. If you have ever patiently endured physical affliction, or responded in love through a difficult marriage, then you have sown in tears.

When you hurt, physically or emotionally, it's hard to muster a patient or godly response. Take heart, for one day God will reward you with sheaves of joy—all because you were faithful through your tears.[133]

JONI EARECKSON TADA

WEEKEND

BUILDING CAREFULLY

By wisdom a house is built,
*   and through understanding it is established;*
through knowledge its rooms are filled
*   with rare and beautiful treasures.*

PROVERBS 24:3-4

As New Testament people, we no longer build a temple for the Lord. Christ dwells not in a temple of stone, but in the lives of his people—lives dedicated for his use. It takes careful thought to build a foundation for life on God's Word. It takes careful thought to frame a life with prayer. It takes constant prioritizing to "seek first his kingdom" (Matthew 6:33) when so many temptations and decisions confront us. But the rewards are worth all the work.

When we provide the "perspiration" to build carefully, Jesus Christ provides the "inspiration." He comes to dwell with us. He "decorates" our lives with joy. His Spirit paints our rooms with the colors of peace, patience, goodness, gentleness, and self-control.[134]

RUTH DE JAGGER

Heavenly Father, my desire is to build a strong foundation
for my life. Decorate my life with joy—the joy
that comes from your Spirit. Amen.

MONDAY

PARTY WELL

*Do not get drunk on wine.... Instead, be filled
with the Spirit. Speak to one another with psalms,
hymns and spiritual songs. Sing and make music
in your heart to the Lord.*

EPHESIANS 5:18–19

We Christians might look a bit more redeemed if we learned more about partying well—finding ways to celebrate the victories and milestones in each other's lives and also celebrating the traditional (and maybe even some untraditional) seasonal holidays and holy days.

Celebrate! I know, putting on a party, even an informal gathering, takes effort, from organizing to cleanup. But I think our society, even our church, is hungry for meaningful interaction. Forget the virtual Internet party. Have a real one that includes smiles, laughter, and popcorn. Let people gather around the grill. Skewer their own shish kebabs. Make their own pizzas. Decorate their own Christmas cookies.

Why not share the goodness of God in your life with others? Gather to celebrate because we are made for community. Celebrate the moment. Set up a milestone. Treasure the memory. Share the joy.[135]

SHEILA WALSH

TUESDAY

HE'S WATCHING OVER YOU

He who watches over you will not slumber; ...
the LORD will watch over your coming and going
both now and forevermore.

PSALM 121:3, 8

Caring is a gift you give another person. And Christian women are good at caring. We cannot always head off disaster. Sometimes we discover that the light at the end of the tunnel really is the headlight of an oncoming train. Even so, I've found that the best thing to hold on to in this life is each other. When even that fails, we can be assured that God is holding on to us.

I try to take the cold water thrown upon me, heat it with enthusiasm, and use the steam to push ahead. I seek to love and to live in the strength of the Lord. At the end of each day, before turning down the covers, I turn all my problems over to the Holy Spirit. I'm grateful he stays up late to handle them. Then I lay down, secure in the knowledge that broken things become blessed things if I let Christ do the mending![136] Then I can go forward in joy.

BARBARA JOHNSON

WEDNESDAY

✳

DON'T MISS THIS!

*Jesus said, "Let your light shine before men,
that they may see your good deeds and praise
your Father in heaven."*

MATTHEW 5:16

I hadn't seen two-year-old Logan in a while, and so spending three days with him was a special treat. I am mesmerized by his chuckle, the sound of his voice, his innocence. At that age, kisses are endless, and hugs happen every five minutes. I loved watching his excitement at the sight of his mom and dad. Every time they came into the room or passed by for something, Logan announced with a glow, "Mommy! Daddy!" as if he was showing them off or telling me, "Don't miss this!"

Watching him, I realized that I wanted to be just like Logan. To have people so taken by my joy, my innocence, and my excitement about my Father. To be so given over to God that all I am reflects my upbringing by him. Jesus: I want to show him off in the holiest sense. When I walk into a room, I want the Holy Spirit to say, "Don't miss this."[137] What a joy!

KATHY TROCCOLI

THURSDAY

❖

LOVE BEYOND MEASURE

*May our Lord Jesus Christ himself and God our Father,
who loved us and by his grace gave us eternal encouragement and good hope, encourage your hearts and
strengthen you in every good deed and word.*

2 THESSALONIANS 2:16—17

If love could be measured, it would be measured by how
much it gives. Would you like to know the extent to which
you love? Then ask yourself: How much do I give? To be
honest, love that gives without limits doesn't even ask that
question. It just joyfully gives without taking any notice of
how much has been sacrificed.

That's how God loves. And the measure of the love of God
is in whom he gave. He gave his Son. His only begotten. He
gave everything, nothing held back, every last ounce, all in all.

That's why God should be so easy to trust. With you, he
never uses words of despair or defeat, hopelessness or frustra-
tion. His encouraging love never mentions fear or failure.
Those aren't words of love. Not his love. When God encourages your heart, he speaks words of hope and victory, rest and
peace, joy and triumph.[138]

JONI EARECKSON TADA

FRIDAY

TRUST HIM WITH *All* YOUR HEART

Trust in the LORD with all your heart
  and lean not on your own understanding;
in all your ways acknowledge him,
  and he will make your paths straight.

PROVERBS 3:5–6

G od uses circumstances, situations, and people to test us. When we face trials and testing, we have a choice. We can trust in ourselves and our earthly resources, or we can trust in the strength of the Lord, which gives us the ability to rejoice regardless of the circumstances.

If you are enduring testing, be aware of the clear choices before you. If you trust in worldly power, wealth, friends or family, neighbors, or your own understanding, you will be disappointed. But King David reminds us: "The LORD is a refuge for the oppressed, a stronghold in times of trouble" (Psalm 9:9).

Put your trust in God. Rely on his strength, and he will fill you with joy, peace, and hope. To the precise extent you are able to trust him, you will be enabled to live in his peace without fear for today or apprehension for the future.[139]

EMILY GARDINER NEAL,
QUOTED BY SUE BUCHANAN

WEEKEND

✦

KNOWING THE ENDING

I am God, and there is no other;
I am God, and there is none like me.
I make known the end from the beginning,
from ancient times, what is still to come.

ISAIAH 46:9–10

My friend Judy and I love to spend time in bookstores. I head for the history section, then move to the children's section. From there, I might glance at cookbooks. But no matter where I wheel in the store, I always know where I can find Judy. She loves mysteries.

When I asked Judy where she picked up her peculiar reading habit, she told me that for her, the suspense wasn't in the conclusion, but in how the writer handled the story. Knowing the ending enhanced the book. Judy is not alone. In the Scripture for today, God says he makes known the end from the beginning. In fact, he's even written in the Bible the very last chapter of history.

I think God makes the end known because he wants to encourage us. And get this: The ending of your story has been declared from the beginning. It reads this way: Jesus wins![140]

JONI EARECKSON TADA

Monday

❖

Lavish Grace

From the fullness of his grace we have all received one blessing after another.

JOHN 1:16

T he word *grace* is now as familiar to me as wind or rain, although it was quite foreign to me until recently. Grace was never meant to be something we nibble on to get us through tough times. It is meant to soak us to (and through) the skin and fill us so full that we can hardly catch our breath.

The joy that springs out of grace is so different from mere happiness. Happy occasions have always helped me forget about the things that make me sad. But the experience of joy is different, deeper, because it knows the whole story. Grace embraced all that was good and true and all that was bad and faithless about me. Grace is love with its eyes wide open.

True grace is so overwhelming you are compelled to extend it to those around you. It takes the initiative to live with passion and compassion; it does not play it safe, but lavishes itself on others, just as grace is daily lavished on us.[141]

SHEILA WALSH

TUESDAY

BEING ORIGINALS

I praise you because I am fearfully and wonderfully made;
  your works are wonderful,
  I know that full well.

PSALM 139:14

I attended a gala occasion recently to which I wore a dressy pants outfit with stylish heels. My hair was fluffed, and my ears were adorned with a new pair of dazzling earrings. I felt spiffy…until I arrived at the event. I was the only woman with slacks on, and I felt awkward. After a considerable period of time, I spotted another gal in slacks, and I wondered if she would want to sit with me and be best friends. Soon several others arrived in similar attire, and I no longer felt the need to bond.

Aren't we women funny? We work hard to be originals and then fear our originality has made us different! I enjoy being center stage unless it's under a critical spotlight. Like the time I spoke, only to learn afterward that my slip was hanging in a southerly direction waving to the onlookers. Despite today's fads, I prefer to keep my underwear undercover. Know what I mean?[142]

PATSY CLAIRMONT

WEDNESDAY

❋

TIME WITH THE SHEPHERD

The LORD is my shepherd, I shall not be in want.

PSALM 23:1

Your day is bursting at the seams. Who has time to just sit before God with no words, no agenda, no schedule? Maybe it's time to make time!

Psalm 23 would be a good place to begin. Imagine Jesus, your Shepherd, leading you into a beautiful pasture near a quiet stream. In this tranquil setting, Jesus refreshes you spiritually. He guides you in his ways and walks with you through even the darkest, most difficult times. You have no need to fear—his authority and power are a comfort to you. He prepares a lavish banquet for you under the shade of the trees. He seats you in a place of honor and sends goodness your way for as long as you live. And with your death will come the joy of living in his presence forever.

Take your wounded, battle-weary heart to Jesus and just sit with him awhile. Take time to bask in God's presence and enjoy who he is and who you are in him.[143]

WOMEN OF FAITH STUDY BIBLE

THURSDAY

THE RHYTHM OF LIFE

Jesus went out to a mountainside to pray,
and spent the night praying to God.

LUKE 6:12

The moon and the ocean both provide exquisite models of the rhythm of life—consistent in their waxing and waning, advance and retreat, ebb and flow. But in our brief earthly journey, most of us just haven't quite been able to get the hang of change. We dread the ebbing, fearing the flow will never return. We demand a constancy that is impossible.

If the joy is in the flow—the moments of great advance, the rush—then the maturing and growing is in the retreat, the pulling back, the ebb, during which there is a grand preparation and anticipation of the next exciting surge forward. The mighty ocean wave retreats to empower its next forward motion.

In God's infinite understanding of the human condition, he reaches out to assuage the dread and fear of change: "Trust me," he says. "I will never leave you. Come to me…and I will give you rest. In my presence is fullness of joy."[144]

JOY MACKENZIE

FRIDAY

HE IS YOUR ROCK

The LORD is my rock, my fortress and my deliverer;
my God is my rock, in whom I take refuge.
He is my shield and the horn of my salvation,
my stronghold.

PSALM 18:2

I n this instant world, we often want microwave solutions to crock-pot problems. I'm not ashamed to admit that I lack solutions to overwhelming troubles. Some things belong to the Lord; he alone knows these secrets. On this earth we seek advice from experts, wisdom from counselors, solace from comforters, encouragement from mentors. But when you get right down to it, the bottom line is that we must trust the Lord through it all.

Jesus is there when nobody else is. Jesus is the only foundation. You are not just a number in a network in cyberspace. There is Someone who knows your face, your name, your need. He never offers platitudes and never patronizes. Instead, he offers love and a place to land. He gives the quiet assurance that he is all you need at any point in life.

Take a chance. Embrace the vision God gives you. Celebrate life.[145] Rejoice!

BARBARA JOHNSON

WEEKEND

✦

SHIELD THE JOYOUS

Let all who take refuge in you be glad;
let them ever sing for joy.
Spread your protection over them,
that those who love your name may rejoice in you.

PSALM 5:11

Joy. It's a powerful force. It looks in the face of life with all its tears and tragedy, all its ups and downs, and it wraps a blanket of eternal comfort around our shoulders. It doesn't leave the scene. This gift the world seeks after and sells its soul to buy—found in the arms of the One who is joy. It has no substance without his presence.

The Book of Common Prayer includes a beautiful prayer for evening: "Tend the sick, Lord Christ, give rest to the weary, bless the dying, soothe the suffering, pity the afflicted, shield the joyous; and all for your love's sake. Amen."

Did you hear it? It's my prayer for you. I tuck it into this page with all the love of heaven: "Shield the joyous."[146]

SHEILA WALSH

Heavenly Father, wrap us up, dear Lord. Keep us safe and
kind and hopeful. Speak to us in the quiet and in the
noise and in all the moments of our days. Amen.

MONDAY

DYING TO LIVE

Jesus said, "If anyone would come after me,
he must deny himself and take up his cross
daily and follow me."

LUKE 9:23

"Taking up your cross" represents many different things in each of our lives. Who wants to go through the dying process? Yet, without the crucifixion, there would have been no resurrection.

We can hold on to things and stay in places of brokenness, go on in ways that are false in healing and peace. And, in doing so, we can suffer the tragedy of missing God's heart.

Or we can lay down our lives to let God do as he wishes. But we are the ones who must put ourselves under the cross so that his blood may pour over our lives. Often we want to avoid this process. I know I do—only to arrive at a place to which the Lord has absolutely no part in bringing me. I look at my person and see holes and flaws that he would gladly fill and fix, if I would just surrender and do it his way. Holiness could then have free reign in me,[147] and I could know the joy of resurrection.

KATHY TROCCOLI

TUESDAY

GETTING TO KNOW ALL OF GOD

I keep asking that the God of our Lord Jesus Christ, the glorious Father, may give you the Spirit of wisdom and revelation, so that you may know him better.

EPHESIANS 1:17

When I think of the Father's special gift to us, I think of his plan of salvation. The Father was the One who came up with the idea. That's why I often spend time worshiping him in reverence and respect.

Other times in my prayers, I think about God the Son and his Father's plan of salvation. And my response is gratitude that he's my Savior and obedience to him as Lord.

When I dwell on the Holy Spirit and his gift of strength and encouragement of heart, I remember that he's the One who gives us assurance and joy. That's why I take care not to grieve, quench, or oppose him.

Father, Son, and Holy Spirit. I am filled to the measure of all the fullness of God as I commune with each member of the Trinity. It's a glorious way to experience a full communion with the Lord, and thereby discover how wide, long, high, and deep is the love of Christ.[148]

JONI EARECKSON TADA

WEDNESDAY

❋

OPEN TO TOMORROW

"I the LORD do not change,"
says the LORD Almighty.

MALACHI 3:6

Like it or not, constant change is part of modern life. But some things don't change, like God's love; friendship with Jesus, his Son; and the power of the Holy Spirit.

When you think you've had just about all the change you can stand, reach out and take one step farther into God's wide arms. Although his love, friendship, and power never change, he made you with a big, elastic spiritual cord that stretches with every tug and pull. He knows exactly how much give it's got. If he's calling you to stretch, he knows you've got what it takes. Reach!

God knows change can make your life richer. Live for today, but hold your hands open to tomorrow. Anticipate the future and its changes with joy. There is a seed of God's love in every event, every circumstance, every unpleasant situation in which you may find yourself. Don't get stuck in a rut or hung up on an outdated blessing. You serve a God of change![149]

BARBARA JOHNSON

THURSDAY

❋

A FEW CLOSE FRIENDS

A friend loves at all times.

I have only a few close friends. We're not talking casual acquaintances here. We're talking people who know me inside out—people I could trade panty hose with, people I can trust with my darkest secrets, my most delicate china, and my wildest dreams. People for whom I don't have to put on makeup or straighten the house.

Only low-maintenance friends qualify for this short list! I can cut short a telephone conversation without explanation; I can NOT invite them to a dinner party, and they know I must have a good reason. They never demand more than I can give and are willing to let me sacrifice for them when they are in need. The give-and-take is joyful and genuine. (I know lots of folks who are exceptionally generous givers but so self-sufficient that they would die before they let a friend return a favor. A good friend is also a gracious receiver!)

Who are your close friends? Have you told them lately how much you appreciate them?[150]

JOY MACKENZIE

FRIDAY

✦

ALL OF ME

May the God who gives us peace make you holy
in every way and keep your whole being—spirit, soul,
and body—free from every fault at the coming of
our Lord Jesus Christ.

1 THESSALONIANS 5:23 GNT

The psalmist David spoke the truth. He faced his fears head-on, and following that authentic path led him to receive the gift of peace. I believe that deep, abiding peace is possible only when all our cards are on the table before the Lord. I'm convinced that we can't be at peace if we are attempting to hide our true selves from God. Facing our deepest fears means making peace with our *seen self* and with our *unseen self.*

I am learning to bring *all* the parts of me into God's presence, into the circle of his embrace, because I have become convinced that this is the only path to peace. This journey has changed my life. Because his mercies are new *every* morning, you can find the courage to bring all of who you are to all of who he is. You can face your fears head-on. You can find the peace that transcends all understanding.[151]

SHEILA WALSH

WEEKEND

❖

No Pleasure in Punishment

*Rid yourselves of all the offenses you have committed,
and get a new heart and a new spirit. Why will you die,
O house of Israel? For I take no pleasure in the death
of anyone, declares the Sovereign LORD. Repent and live!*

EZEKIEL 18:31–32

My father used to say it hurt him to smack my backside with a spoon as much as it hurt me (I strongly doubted that at the time). However, what parent hasn't experienced anger over the disobedience of a child? It goes wrong when that anger energizes the spanking. Some parents feel self-satisfaction in reaching for the rod.

God is different. We can say for certain that our heavenly Father never takes delight in punishing his children. He gets no kick from it. His anger is not quenched by it. He gains no satisfaction in it. So what energizes him when it comes to discipline? Our training. We are not his whipping post, no matter what our sin. We are his children, and he wants us to share in his holiness. It is in this that he takes delight.[152]

JONI EARECKSON TADA

*Thank you, God, for disciplining me with your strong and
holy hand. Because of it, I will share in your holiness.
Thank you for keeping me in training. Amen.*

Monday

Faith That Blesses

Those who have faith are blessed along with Abraham, the man of faith.

GALATIANS 3:9

The other day I spent many long moments by the window, feeling a little blue, hoping to see a few birds. Suddenly the bird feeder was abuzz with new and different friends. Finches flew out of nowhere, a mockingbird showed up, a couple of red-breasted robins hopped by to join the party, and two doves perched on a nearby fence to wait their turn for the birdseed.

I sat there wide-eyed and smiling. Without thinking, I exclaimed, "Thank you, Lord, for the birds!" It struck me that the entire backyard party was organized by the Lord himself. When I needed a lift, he brought by an array of brightly colored, happy birds. Doves and robins don't drop in by chance—if the Lord notices when a sparrow falls, then surely he directs their flight paths.

It's a matter of faith—faith to observe God's hand in everything that happens. Faith to believe that the flashing wings of a blue jay fluttering across the yard is a gift personally orchestrated by the Lord.[153]

JONI EARECKSON TADA

TUESDAY

✦

ENTERING INTO JOY

Where the Spirit of the Lord is, there is freedom.

2 CORINTHIANS 3:17

In *A Grief Observed*, C.S. Lewis tells of an experience his wife had—before they married. One morning she felt "haunted" by what she felt was God "demanding her attention." Lewis continues, "Not being a perfected saint, she had the feeling that it would be a question, as it usually is, of some unrepented sin or tedious duty. At last she gave in—and faced him. But the message was, 'I want to give you something,' and instantly she entered into joy."

As long as you hold on to basic faulty definitions of who you are, you won't find the joy. As long as you try to win God's approval, or prove to him that you're "worthy" of anything, the joy will be just out of your reach.

What liberation can be found in the ashes of life, when you finally discover who God is, who you are, and who God wants you to be.[154]

SHEILA WALSH

WEDNESDAY

❁

JOYFUL IN HOPE

Be joyful in hope, patient in affliction, faithful in prayer.

ROMANS 12:12

Why does God say to be joyful in hope? Think about it. The focus of our hope is yet to be fulfilled; we don't yet possess that for which we hope. And you'll agree that it's hard to be joyful about something we don't yet have!

One day, while lying in bed, it hit home that God wants me to be joyful about future things. Just as we have the command to be faithful in prayer and patient in affliction, we have a command to be joyful in hope. How can God command joy? It's easy once we realize what's over the heavenly horizon.

Does the idea of heavenly glories above put a smile on your face? Do you get a charge when you talk about the return of the Lord? Words like *pleasure*, *happiness*, and *delight* should come to mind when you hope in the Lord. Heaven will seem more near and real to you as you stir up your joy over that for which you hope.[155]

JONI EARECKSON TADA

THURSDAY

✦

JOY IS A CHOICE

*Let us fix our eyes on Jesus, the author and
perfecter of our faith, who for the joy set before him
endured the cross, scorning its shame, and sat down
at the right hand of the throne of God.*

HEBREWS 12:2

J oy is not only an emotion to be desired, it is also a command to be obeyed. Joy is—to some degree—a choice.
How can this be? Are you to simply ignore your circumstances? No, but a life of joy can be learned—and suffering is
most often the teacher.

The Scriptures clearly point out the path toward a life of
joy: Accept your circumstances and be thankful in them;
choose not to worry; fix your eyes on Jesus rather than on
your situation—follow his example in suffering—and put
your hope in future glory. It is through the joy and peace
exhibited in suffering that God is most visible in your life.
When you live a life of joy—regardless of your circumstances—others will see Jesus in you.

Whatever your current circumstances, God longs to comfort you, heal you, and give you his peace, joy, and hope. Fix
your eyes on Jesus, and live life in joy and peace.[156]

WOMEN OF FAITH STUDY BIBLE

FRIDAY

COMMITTED TO
PRAY FOR OTHERS

*I urge, then, first of all, that requests, prayers,
intercession and thanksgiving be made for everyone.*

1 TIMOTHY 2:1

The promise to pray for someone going through hard times rolls easily off our tongues. Our sisters, brothers, and children in the faith need our committed involvement in their lives. We never know why some things happen as they do. But we stand upon the rocky shores of life and keep on praying, because prayer changes the one who prays as much as it changes those for whom we pray.

Some people think their prayers have fallen on deaf ears. But they have not. It takes faith to know that. Faith is the ability to let your light shine even after your fuse is blown. Faith is seeing light with the eyes of your heart, when the eyes of your body see only darkness ahead.

God is changing things through our willingness to pray and keep at it. While sorrow looks back and worry looks around, faith looks up. As we pray, we may face finite disappointment, but we must never lose infinite hope[157]—or joy.

BARBARA JOHNSON

WEEKEND

❋

LOOK FOR HIM IN THE
LITTLE THINGS

*"You will seek me and find me when you seek me with
all your heart. I will be found by you," declares the LORD.*

JEREMIAH 29:13-14

S ome people hate answering machines. But traveling as
much as I do, I find them not only necessary, but often
comforting. The messages that end with, "Please know I'm
praying for you," or, "Been thinking about you," or, "I love
you," seem to come at just the right time. Little gifts that
soothe my soul at the end of long, difficult days.

I believe that God is in our everyday lives, no matter
whether we see him, feel him, or hear him. Many moments
occur in our lives that reveal his face, his touch, his voice.
Look for him today. He will be found. You will be sweetly surprised at the many ways he surrounds you with his love.[158] Just
thinking about it, makes me rejoice!

KATHY TROCCOLI

*Heavenly Father, I know you are near, always at work
in my life, always looking out for my best interest.
As I seek you with my whole heart, open my eyes
to see you in the little things. Amen.*

MONDAY

GOD'S GREENHOUSE

The LORD God took the man and put him in the
Garden of Eden to work it and take care of it.

GENESIS 2:15

Why the gardening mania? Why the books, calendars, accessories, decorations, tools, music, picture frames, furniture, clothes? Why are we so enchanted with white picket fences made into tables and chairs and head-boards for the bed? Why the silk grapevines, sweet peas, and ficus trees for the bathroom, kitchen, and hall? Because we crave the sweet serenity of greens and golds and deep brown earth. Because fellowship with God began in a garden, and we long for that time and place. Because leaves quivering in the wind, blossoms nodding, grass ruffled by a breeze, remind us of our real home and the peaceful destiny awaiting us. Because when I cheer up with my geraniums, smile at my pansies, laugh with my petunias, they teach me about God's big greenhouse bursting with joy.

Take the seedlings on loan from heaven and share the growth. Get your gloves muddy, your face tanned, and your knees crinkled here on earth. God will make something beautiful out of your effort and energy.[159]

BARBARA JOHNSON

TUESDAY

❋

THE EYES OF CHRIST

God demonstrates his own love for us in this:
While we were still sinners, Christ died for us.

ROMANS 5:8

We frequently feel pulled in a dozen different directions, pressured by contemporary role models who encourage us to look at a job or our looks as the central core of our identity—when our greatest joy and highest privilege as believers is designed to come from knowing, serving, and loving our Lord.

As we seek to serve our Savior and humbly live according to his unduplicatable design for our lives, we see that our self-worth is based on God's view of us, not on our own opinions or others' attitudes toward us. Our identity becomes securely centered in the reality of what Jesus has accomplished on our behalf, not on what we have accomplished for ourselves.

Proclaiming the Lord's love often requires a sacrifice of our personal ease. It takes courage, time, and effort. It takes an ardent desire to view creation with the eyes of Christ.[160]

DEBORAH EVANS

WEDNESDAY

❖

GOD WORKS EVERYTHING OUT FOR YOUR GOOD

We know that in all things God works
for the good of those who love him,
who have been called according to his purpose.

ROMANS 8:28

—Night is drawing nigh—
For all that has been—Thanks!
To all that shall be—Yes!

These challenging words were found in a manuscript of Dag Hammarskjöld, Secretary-General of the United Nations from 1953 until his death in an airplane crash in 1961.

When I look closely at what he wrote, there is more there than I can wrap my heart around. I believe he is saying that for every single thing that has happened in our lives, we can learn to say with confidence, even joy, "Not my will, but yours be done." I certainly don't believe he is suggesting that all the pain in our lives is inflicted by God to see if he can squeeze a heart-broken yes out of us. But I do embrace the mystery that, in the darkest valleys, even when saying yes will break our hearts, the light of the world is with us, and we will come to know him, to live and trust him, in ways we never have before.[161]

SHEILA WALSH

THURSDAY

❋

A LISTENING FRIEND

Jesus said, "Trust in God; trust also in me."

JOHN 14:1

Our heavenly Father gives us inexpressible comfort and privilege. He gives us a safe place to talk frankly with him—a place to bring our doubts and our dilemmas. We don't need to measure words or weigh thoughts. We can just pour out our frustrated hearts to God—chaff and grain together. We can go to him with our anger, our questions, our lack of understanding, our fury.

He listens. He loves. He reads our hearts and understands our frustrations. He understands the grief and sorrow we feel when our loved ones die. He understands our anger when doctors make fatal medical mistakes on those we love. We can safely, without fear, go to him with our complaints, our criticisms, our hostilities.

He is our friend—the friend who never takes offense or gets his feelings hurt or turns his back to us. We can talk to him in complete confidence, never worrying that our secrets will be shared or ridiculed or used against us. In his faithful way, he listens to us. With great love, he answers our prayers in the way he deems best. We may not understand his answers. But we can joyfully trust in his decisions.[162]

DENISE GEORGE

FRIDAY

A LITTLE BUBBLE OF JOY

Let the peace of Christ rule in your hearts....
And be thankful.

COLOSSIANS 3:15

E very day I thank God for good health and good eyesight
and an abundance of energy. The joy I have is a gift, too.
That little bubble of joy that comes up from inside me; it's
always there, and I just praise the Lord for it.

Every day I thank God for the gift of laughter and the ability
to find the fun in the midst of tragic situations. You see, one
laugh equals three spoons of oat bran, and one hearty chuckle
burns up six calories. So I praise the Lord that he's given me a
funny bone. Without a sense of humor, I'd be a lot heavier, not
to mention sadder!

Practice thankfulness every day. Look for the humor in
every difficult circumstance. (If you don't see it right away,
that usually means it's sneaking up on you.)[163] And ask God
to give you a little bubble of joy—you'll be glad you did!

BARBARA JOHNSON

WEEKEND

ONE HOPEFUL STEP

God hath not given us the spirit of fear; but of power,
and of love, and of a sound mind.

2 TIMOTHY 1:7 KJV

In his book *Essentials*, Jean Toomer uses a great simile to describe the power fear can have—if we let it: "Fear is a noose that binds until it strangles." It strangles the joy from our lives. It strangles any hope we have for a bright future. It strangles our ability to step out and take the risks that will open up healthy relationships with others. That noose can be cut, and we can be set free.

But you may be afraid to let go of your fear. If so, I again challenge you just to stop. Take a deep breath—and let it out. Let that breath be your very first step toward letting go. Look at one positive "what if": What if you chose to cut the noose? What if you chose to take one hopeful step that in so doing you could know the joy of the Lord?[164]

SHEILA WALSH

Heavenly Father, you haven't given me a spirit of fear.
Today I choose to let it go. Amen.

166   PROMISES OF JOY

MONDAY

❋

HEED GOOD ADVICE

Fools think their own way is right,
but the wise listen to advice.

PROVERBS 12:15 NRSV

I had been invited for a horseback ride. My husband didn't think me wise to accept. His cautions rang in my ears as I headed out. The only challenge I had was my stirrups. They were a little too long for my short legs, and I felt like a toe dancer as I stretched to keep my feet in the stirrups.

About six minutes into the ride, my leg muscles began to scream. Finally, with my legs stretched far beyond their designed reach and with a kink in my back, I pleaded my cause with the staff. They compassionately headed for the stable. My legs wobbled as I toddled my way to a bench. For three days, my back felt like the horse had ridden me.

Do you find it difficult to take good advice? To live within your limitations? Just remember, if you get a backache from carrying your horse, don't be surprised.[165] Why not listen to sound advice? You're a lot less likely to lose your joy.

PATSY CLAIRMONT

TUESDAY

LAUGHING YOURSELF
TO SLEEP

A cheerful heart enjoys a good time that never ends.

PROVERBS 15:15 NIRV

Sometimes, when I can't sleep, I lie in bed, and instead of counting sheep, I count all the fun people God has put in my life.

On one such occasion, I'd gone to bed at 10:30 P.M. When I woke up, I was sure it was morning, but the clock on my bedside table said it was only 12:30 A.M. I slipped out of bed, went downstairs, made some hot tea, and switched on the TV. But at 3:30 A.M., I went back upstairs, determined to fall asleep.

That's when I remembered some of the stories [my friends] Luci, Patsy, and Marilyn tell, and I started to laugh. I don't know if you've ever felt like laughing while the person next to you is fast asleep, but it makes you laugh even more.

Who can make you giggle and snort just thinking about them and their antics? The next time you can't sleep, thank God for all those who bring joy to your life![166]

SHEILA WALSH

WEDNESDAY

❋

CELEBRATE LIFE

*Whatever you do, work at it with all your heart,
as working for the Lord.*

E very good life is a balance of duty and bliss. We have to
weigh decisions by mind and spirit and by the Word of
God. So make each year count. Instead of clutching it fast,
give it away. "Cast your bread upon the waters" (Ecclesiastes
11:1), and it comes back pretzels!

Do you have a gift for making people laugh? Writing a
short story? Baking a great loaf of bread? Do you listen well?
Throw a mean softball? Can you organize anything with flair?
Are you good at making money? Selling just about anything?
Running a race? Put yourself in the center ring. Offer your
energy to life, and do it heartily, unto the Lord.

Don't forget to celebrate anything you can think of. Do
things that make you aware of how great it is to be alive. Every
day is worth a party, not just the cookie-cutter moments.
Special occasions are everywhere. Don't always be practical
and expedient. God has given us license to be outrageously
happy, friendly, and rejoicing.[167]

BARBARA JOHNSON

THURSDAY

LOOK, LISTEN, HEAR

Deep calls to deep
in the roar of your waterfalls;
all your waves and breakers
have swept over me.
By day the LORD directs his love,
at night his song
is with me—a prayer to the God of my life.

PSALM 42:7–8

The ocean is a favorite place of mine, and I have been there many times. I love to stare into the darkness of a midnight blue sky and listen to sounds that only the waves can make.

When my mind is stayed on Jesus, when my eyes look toward eternal things, I hear the ocean sing. But the sound of this ocean is, oh, so much deeper, so much wider, so much more divine. I begin to see above and beyond my situation and my circumstances to my Savior—his words, his tenderness, his compassion, his ways. My concerns and worries are far less burdensome at the thought and the sight of him.

He lives, and his love is never ending. Look, listen, and hear. God is near. He will bring you perfect peace.[168] He will make your heart sing.

KATHY TROCCOLI

FRIDAY

INDUSTRY OF THE HEART

Who can find a virtuous woman?
for her price is far above rubies.

PROVERBS 31:10 KJV

Women have always been able to make do with what life hands them, to create an ordered universe in the midst of chaos and stress. Women have always been able to make something from nothing: stretching the stew; making the worn-out clothes or opportunities into something new; smiling and caressing in spite of their own inclinations to give in to tears and fatigue; mothering the world. Yet while their hands were performing the task at hand, their minds were racing on. Assimilating. Analyzing. Philosophizing.

So much of men's thinking is applied directly to their work. The result of their thinking is output, income, product. But much of what women think about does not create tangible product. Instead, they ponder the meaning and quality of life. Such pondering may not result in consumable products, but it can produce great souls who ask why instead of merely what and how. Women, after all, are about the industry of the heart.[169] Make it your quest to fulfill your role with joy.

GLORIA GAITHER

WEEKEND

✸

DEADLINES, DEADBEATS, AND DEAD ENDS

You, O LORD, have delivered my soul from death,
my eyes from tears,
    my feet from stumbling,
that I may walk before the LORD
    in the land of the living.

PSALM 116:8–9

Deadlines scream: "Finish that paper." "Fax this letter." "Make that sale." Get it done! Get it out!! Now!!!

Deadbeats clamor: An overbearing boss. A rebellious child. An angry spouse. On my nerves, in my face, at my door.

Dead ends loom: The money is gone. The marriage has failed. The cancer is back. No hope. No way out. It's over. It's done. But God has promised us victory over hopelessness. He assured Peter of a new birth into a living hope that would never fade. He sealed our claim to abundant life in his Son, Jesus.

God's got it under control. His hope is too real to deny. His joy is irrepressible.[170]

JONI EARECKSON TADA

Heavenly Father, I am never without hope because
you are the God of hope. Fill me with all joy and peace
in believing that I may abound in hope. Amen.

MONDAY

YOU CAN TRUST HIM

The LORD is my light and my salvation—
whom shall I fear?
The LORD is the stronghold of my life—
of whom shall I be afraid?

PSALM 27:1

To take comfort in these words I have to trust the Lord—or they are meaningless. But if, like David, I can find myself on my knees with these words on my lips, I will also say with him:

I am still confident of this:
I will see the goodness of the LORD
in the land of the living.
Wait for the LORD;
be strong and take heart
and wait for the LORD.

PSALM 27:13–14[171]

SHEILA WALSH

Heavenly Father, thank you that when everything around
me seems to be in turmoil and chaos, you are my light and
my salvation. Instead of allowing fear to overwhelm me, I
put my trust in you, knowing that I will see your goodness
in the land of the living. I am strong in you and take heart
in your promises. Fill me with your joy. Amen.

TUESDAY

❋

JUST DO IT

Christ's love compels us.

2 CORINTHIANS 5:14

Sometimes the very desire for action leads to the neglect of action. We're so busy searching for the perfect opportunity, the most effective method, the favorable moment, that we not only disqualify ourselves for the mission and miss the joy, but an urgent need is left unanswered.

I have often experienced the pull of an inner voice, urging me to call a friend who is in need. Invariably, I address that urge by checking my watch to see if the time is appropriate, or by mentally reprioritizing my schedule to accommodate a more convenient arrangement.

Born of genuine concern for my friend, my determination to provide the most propitious response thwarts the entire effort. The perfect moment never arrives; there is never a convenient time.

When my friend most needed simply to hear a reassuring voice, I wasn't available. I was busy rearranging God's schedule. Are you, too?[172]

Be quick to obey those inner promptings and experience the joy of being used by God.

JOY MACKENZIE

WEDNESDAY

❋

SPLASHES OF JOY

May my meditation be pleasing to him
as I rejoice in the LORD.

PSALM 104:34

Splashes of joy are all around us—but we have to look for them with joyful eyes. For example, at the post office, I see more than just rows of mailboxes and a long line of people with sagging faces waiting at the counter. On my way in, I look at the cement sidewalk and see millions of little sparkles. When the sun hits the cement just the right way, the sidewalk shines with a million transient diamonds. They make me think of all the blessings God has given me, all the places in my life he wants me to find his blessings, and all the people he has brought into my life.

The smallest things bring me bountiful joy, even brief messages left on my answering machine. A woman who writes to us regularly and supports our ministry called and left this quip on my machine: "Barb, may the joy-bells of heaven ding-dong in your heart today!" It was a gift that splashed joy on an otherwise ordinary day.[173]

BARBARA JOHNSON

THURSDAY

❋

HAPPINESS AND JOY

The precepts of the LORD are right,
giving joy to the heart.

Many people confuse happiness and joy. Happiness is a temporary feeling of pleasure or contentment that fluctuates according to your outward circumstances. Buying a new car, for example, may make you happy, but when it breaks down, you aren't so happy anymore. The Bible speaks of a permanent feeling of pleasure or contentment that emanates from within and is based in a person's relationship with God. The Bible refers to this as joy. It's never-changing because God is never-changing. It's one of the evidences of his presence in your life.

Try this: Take a look at your life. Does your sense of pleasure and contentment fluctuate with your circumstances? Or do you have a deep, inner sense of pleasure and contentment that flows out of a personal relationship with God? If you find that you possess mere happiness rather than joy, open your heart to a relationship with God. He's waiting with open arms.[174]

MICHAEL J. FOSTER

176 PROMISES OF JOY

FRIDAY

JOY FROM A DIFFERENT ANGLE

God has arranged the parts in the body,
every one of them, just as he wanted them to be.
If they were all one part, where would the body be?

1 CORINTHIANS 12:18–19

M en have such a different angle of seeing the joy in things than women. We girls call to others to come see a playful puppy, a snuggly kitten, or a cooing baby. Meanwhile the guys dangle a grass snake like a charm bracelet, point out the newest road kill, and burp loud enough to register 6.3 on the Richter scale.

That's not to say all guys—just a fair portion—go for the yucky stuff of life. But I find that the he-men in my vicinity would rather investigate a spider's nest than check out the new lace curtains. Even though we did start out in the same Garden, we don't seem to be smelling the same rosebush.

We need to respect our differences and to value each other's contribution. Our differences enable us to enlarge each other's angle of viewing life. Treasure each other's uniqueness, and remember to look at life from another angle now and then.[175]

PATSY CLAIRMONT

WEEKEND

❖

NOT A DRESS REHEARSAL

Moses said, "Be strong and courageous. Do not be afraid or terrified because of them, for the LORD your God goes with you; he will never leave you nor forsake you."

Courage and fear. Those two attributes are strange bed-mates. It would seem impossible to experience both of them at the same time; yet I believe that's the challenge of the Christian life. Fear tells us that life is unpredictable, but courage replies quietly, "Yes, but God is in control."

If we will stop for a moment during our cluttered lives to reflect, we will realize that this life is not a rehearsal. This is it. How will we choose to live?

I want to live a passionate life. I want to live a life that recognizes the fears but moves forward with courage. I want to show the world the eternal mystery of what God can do through a miserable sinner who is sold out to him. Why would I settle for anything less? Life is tough, but God is faithful.[176]

SHEILA WALSH

Heavenly Father, there are plenty of things that I could be afraid of, but I choose to trust you. Strengthen my heart that I may be bold and courageous. Amen.

178 PROMISES OF JOY

MONDAY

GET REAL

*Jesus said, "You are the light of the world. A city on a
hill cannot be hidden. Neither do people light a lamp
and put it under a bowl. Instead they put it on its
stand, and it gives light to everyone in the house."*

MATTHEW 5:14–15

I f we want to spread hope and joy, if we want people to
know Jesus Christ, let's stop faking who we are. The only
thing that's separating them from us is that we are forgiven.
Our problems are no less tragic. Our lives no less complicated. Our burdens no less heavy. The difference is that
Christians have Someone who will go the distance with them.

You may be the only Jesus someone else will ever meet.
Be real and involved with people. They may be closer to the
kingdom of heaven than you think. It's in the darkest places,
after all, that the grace of God shines most brightly. That is
where people begin to see him. By our scars we are recognized as belonging to him.

Ask the Holy Spirit to help you be genuine in all your relationships. And allow God to answer the world's questions
through your life.[177] You possess the Source of joy they are
looking for.

BARBARA JOHNSON

TUESDAY

REJOICE WITH OTHERS—
YOUR DAY WILL COME

As it is written:
"No eye has seen,
no ear has heard,
no mind has conceived
what God has prepared for those who love him."

1 CORINTHIANS 2:9

God has made you unique. Resist the attitude that causes you to feel sorrow or betrayal because of someone else's gifts or good fortune. God can come freely into a heart that is generous toward others, into a soul that celebrates the blessings and opportunities others enjoy.

He has intentions for you, a destiny that was ordered at the beginning of time, and he will not withhold it. The Lord is always at work on your behalf, yearning for you to be where *he* desires for you to be.

Keep looking to him, trusting in him. He is always leading you to a higher place—so let him. You may feel lost, far behind, or confused. But if you follow Jesus, it will be the right road, and in the end, you will have peace. For true peace is found only in the center of God's will.[178]

KATHY TROCCOLI

WEDNESDAY

❋

FILLED WITH DELIGHT

I was filled with delight day after day,
rejoicing always in his presence,
rejoicing in his whole world
and delighting in mankind.

PROVERBS 8:30–31

Boredom can rob a person of joy. Apathy may not sink my boat, but it can becalm me and cause despair as the wind is taken out of the sails of my life. Because Christ lives in us, we can be filled with delight day after day. And those things that can and will delight us have nothing to do with position or ministry or fascinating things to do. We can have delight in the dull, monotonous months, in the routine, mundane days, in the lean, hungry years.

Three things will bring rejoicing to our souls: (1) God's very presence, (2) his world around us, and (3) other people! God's promise to be present with us can always bring us comfort and delight. So can the complexity and variety of his creation: a flower, the misty rain, the billowing clouds. Sometimes we may have to look hard at some of the people we encounter, but as we ask, God will help us delight in them, too.[179]

CAROLE MAYHALL

THURSDAY

✺

ENJOY THE DAY

Guide me in your truth and teach me,
for you are God my Savior,
and my hope is in you all day long.

PSALM 25:5

Recently I stopped for breakfast at the local pancake house. I intended to steal a moment to be alone before the day began and its many demands crowded my time.

"Just an egg and a homemade biscuit," I told the waitress, "And a coffee, please." I handed back the menu and turned to the book I'd brought to jumpstart my mind.

I had barely finished the second page before she returned with my breakfast. She poured the coffee and asked if there'd be anything else. "No, I'm fine, thank you," I answered.

She smiled. "Enjoy!" she said, then hurried back to deliver someone else's order.

I've heard a lot of sermons in my day, but the best sermon I'd heard in a long time was preached in one word by a busy waitress as she poured a cup of coffee. It was a choice she had offered me. I could go through this day oblivious to the miracles all around me, or I could tune in and "enjoy!"[180]

GLORIA GAITHER

Friday

God's Wonderful Word

Open my eyes, so that I may behold
wondrous things out of your law.

PSALM 119:18 NRSV

BOOK OF JOY

Open to me words of wisdom in the midst of life's dark days,
Take away my human blindness, give me eyes to see your ways.
I am weak without your goodness, I am lost without
your light.
Word of God, sweet breath of heaven,
Shine upon this child tonight.

Open to me words of kindness when my heart is sad within,
Help me rise above the sorrow, singing songs of joy again.
I will lift my voice to worship, thankful for your gift of grace.
Word of peace, sweet breath of heaven,
Friend until I see your face.

Open now the halls of heaven to each child who seeks
your face,
Mercy flowing like a river from the Christ who took our place.
Took our guilt and shame upon him, bore our pain
upon the tree.
Word of life, sweet breath of heaven,
Love of every love to me.[181]

SHEILA WALSH

WEEKEND

SONGS OF CONQUEST

After consulting the people,
Jehoshaphat appointed men to sing to the LORD
and to praise him for the splendor of his holiness
as they went out at the head of the army, saying:
  "Give thanks to the LORD,
  for his love endures forever."

2 CHRONICLES 20:21

Anyone who spends time with me knows how much I enjoy singing, especially at work. When someone helps me type, we'll reach for the hymnal next to my computer, flip it open to an old favorite, and harmonize our hearts out.

All this is not just to fill the office corridors with song. For me, singing is a wonderful way to clear the spiritual air.

If you're fighting darkness or engaged in a spiritual conflict, if the enemy is poised and ready to attack, the best defense is to sing. It's a way of resisting the devil. Singing is also the best offense. Songs of praise will confuse the enemy and send the devil's hoards hightailing. So pick a hymn, any hymn. Victory over the enemy and clean, clear spiritual air can be yours for a song.[182]

JONI EARECKSON TADA

Heavenly Father, thank you for the weapon of praise
that you have given me to clear the spiritual air
and to put the devil on the run. Amen.

MONDAY

❋

A RIVER OF JOY

The Lamb at the center of the throne will be their shepherd;
he will lead them to springs of living water.
And God will wipe away every tear from their eyes.

REVELATION 7:17

S in and pain seem to prevail. Babies die of cancer. Puppies are hit on the road. We yell at our children. The power of suffering is that great. So, what, in the end, does the cross really mean? The answer, in part, is that the cross never promises to free us from pain and suffering, not at least in the present. The cross, in fact, promises just the opposite: the certainty of pain and suffering.

Christianity, alone among the world's religions, does not run from pain but embraces it, and then and only then, moves through it. Through the sorrow of the world, through that certain fog of doubt and pain, we have faith: sure of what we hope for, certain of what we do not see. God is love. God is in control. God will wipe away every tear and replace it with a river of joy.[183]

DEFORIA LANE

TUESDAY

THE FINGERPRINTS OF GOD

We love him, because he first loved us.

1 JOHN 4:19 KJV

I see God's fingerprints in his handiwork: a sunrise, a shooting star, a lilac bush, and a newborn's smile. I observe a measure of his strength in a hurricane, an earthquake, a thunderbolt. I see his creativity in a kangaroo, the Grand Canyon, and a blue-eyed, red-headed baby. I detect his humor in a porpoise, a cactus, and a two-year-old's twinkling eyes. I am aware of his mysteriousness when I consider the Trinity, the solar system, and his desire to be in communion with us.

But how do we find God? How do we take hold of his humor, his joy? Sometimes we search him out, and sometimes he "finds" us. Every time we think of God, it is because he first had us on his mind. The Lord is always the initiator. He has been from the beginning, and he will be to the end. So know that once you have invited him to enter your life, you are on his mind, and he is in your heart.[184]

PATSY CLAIRMONT

WEDNESDAY

✦

YOU CAN CHOOSE

In your anger do not sin;
when you are on your beds,
search your hearts and be silent.

PSALM 4:4

"Did you mail that insurance form, sweetie?" I asked Barry one afternoon.

He seemed to lose a little color. "I forgot," he said.

I found myself standing on the edge of a cliff and knew I had to choose whether I would dive off or back off. I asked Barry to excuse me for a moment, and I made a conscious, determined choice to get on my knees and to let my anger go. As I released my fury, I was filled with joy.

Choosing to let go of my tempestuous responses may not seem big to you, but it's making a huge difference in our lives. I want to be the fragrance of Christ in the midst of the storms of life, not part of the storm front.

If you struggle with old behaviors, I encourage you to invite Christ into the moment and to let those old patterns go. You can choose. You can be a drop of rain or a ray of sunshine.[185]

SHEILA WALSH

THURSDAY

✦

OUR SHEPHERD
DELIGHTS IN US

Jesus said, "I am the good shepherd. The good shepherd lays down his life for the sheep."

JOHN 10:11

When I say, "The Lord is my shepherd," I remember that he has charge over my life. As my shepherd, he watches over me to see that I stay in the fold. He loves me unconditionally in spite of my going my own willful way sometimes. He protects me from danger. He provides everything for me. He chastises me when I do wrong. He comforts me when I am distressed. He bandages my wounds when I get hurt. He calms my fears when I am afraid. He takes care of my relationships when they become shaky. He bathes me in his Spirit when I seek his face. He communicates with me in ways I can understand.

God promises to provide for all of our needs according to his riches in glory in Christ Jesus. I know he will do that. And he often delights in giving us what we want, too.[186] We bring joy to God just as surely as God brings joy to us.

THELMA WELLS

FRIDAY

BE A HOPE BRINGER

Always be prepared to give an answer to everyone who asks you to give the reason for the hope that you have.

1 PETER 3:15

One woman went to her doctor to get the results of a checkup. The doctor said, "I have good news and bad news. Which do you want first?"

She answered, "The good news!"

The doctor said, "You have twenty-four hours to live."

"Good grief!" exclaimed the woman. "That's the good news? Then what's the bad news?"

"The bad news," replied the doctor, "is that I was supposed to tell you yesterday."

Don't let your life speed out of control. Live intentionally. Slice out time from your schedule to do something today that will last beyond your lifetime.

Commit yourself to being a hope bringer, no matter what. Hope looks for the good in people, opens doors for people, discovers what can be done to help, lights a candle, does not yield to cynicism. Hope sets people free. Find creative ways to pass it on to someone else.[187] It will fill your heart with joy.

BARBARA JOHNSON

WEEKEND

THE JOY OF CHRIST RISEN

God loves a cheerful giver. And God is able
to make all grace abound to you, so that in
all things at all times, having all that you need,
you will abound in every good work.

2 CORINTHIANS 9:7–8

Joy is prayer. Joy is strength. Joy is love. Joy is a net of love by which you can catch souls. God loves a cheerful giver. One gives most who gives with joy. The best way to show our gratitude to God and people is to accept everything with joy. A joyful heart is the normal result of a heart burning with love. Never let anything so fill you with sorrow as to make you forget the joy of Christ risen.

This I tell my sisters. This I tell to you.[188]

MOTHER TERESA OF CALCUTTA

Heavenly Father, I rejoice because Jesus is risen! The more I
think about it, the more my heart is filled with joy. Lead me
to others who need to hear this good news. Nothing is
impossible or hopeless now because Jesus triumphed over
death, hell, and the grave. I am a cheerful giver of these
glad tidings and count it a privilege to share your joy with
others. Use me to shine your light in the darkness. Amen.

MONDAY

✦

HIS BEST IS OURS TO HAVE

In him we were also chosen, having been predestined according to the plan of him who works out everything in conformity with the purpose of his will.

EPHESIANS 1:11

Why is it so difficult for us to understand that God only wants the best for us? Why is it so hard to take him at his Word? His promises can never be broken. They have withstood the test of time.

Next time you think you hear nothing in response to your prayers, don't assume that God isn't listening. He may simply want you to rest in his shadow until he reveals his answer. When you hear a direct no, remind yourself there will always be a better yes.

I pray that we will both grow in our faith. That the times we doubt God will grow fewer and fewer and that the eyes of our hearts will be enlightened. That we may know God's goodness, real and solid, even in the darkness. He only wants the best, and his best is ours to have.[189] The joy we experience when he showers us with his blessing will make the wait well worth it.

KATHY TROCCOLI

TUESDAY

SHARING TIMES

Each one of you also must love his wife as he loves himself, and the wife must respect her husband.

EPHESIANS 5:33

Many women have told me that intimate communication with their husbands—special times of togetherness—after the children are in bed, during the day on the telephone, at breakfast, at dinner, or at a restaurant over a cup of coffee, are the most enjoyable part of a woman's day.

When my wife and I get together to talk, we use a concept called the "revolving method" of communication. It involves four steps:

I ask my wife to share her feelings or thoughts with me.

I respond by rephrasing what I think she said.

She answers either yes or no.

If she answers no, I continue to rephrase what I think she said until I get a yes response.

My wife goes through the same four steps when I am explaining my feelings to her.

This process has nearly eliminated misinterpretations and greatly increased the joy in our marriage.[190]

GARY SMALLEY

WEDNESDAY

✦

HE LOVES YOU,
JUST AS YOU ARE

*I pray that your love will have deep roots. I pray that
it will have a strong foundation. May you have power
with all God's people to understand Christ's love.
May you know how wide and long and high and deep it is.*

EPHESIANS 3:17–18 NIRV

In an article entitled "The Secret Self," Mike Yaconelli says, "Somewhere in the side streets of the soul is a place where secret self lives." How many times have you thought, *If people really knew me…?* The great irony is that we imagine we can keep the secret part of our soul disguised from God. What I love about Yaconelli's article is its conclusion. He imagines Dietrich Bonhoeffer walking from self-doubt and martyrdom all the way home: He "walks confidently into the open arms of his God who, it turns out, is a friend to Bonhoeffer's secret self…*as well as* to the self everyone admired."

This is radical and wonderful. God knows all that is true about us and is a friend both to the face we show and to the face we hide. He does not love us less for our human weaknesses.[191] What great joy there is in being known and loved by him, just as we are.

SHEILA WALSH

THURSDAY

❂

COLLECTIBLES

Love one another deeply, from the heart.

1 PETER 1:22

Mother loves to philosophize. "We humans are real packrats," she once said. "We hold on to the past for dear life." She leaned forward in her chair: "We're not limited just to fine china and snapshots or old leather-bound books. All our lives, we are making collections that are far more significant…fears, phobias, and suspicions…hopes, dreams, and illusions…attributes, persuasions, and prejudices."

As a result of our conversation, I am learning to discard the redundancies of my life. I would be willing to give up nearly every collection I have, except one—my family and friends. They are truly a part of my life that gives me warmth, color, and texture; courage, comfort, and strength; joy, tears, and very often, laughter in large doses!

If I were asked what I cherish most, my answer would surely be my faith in God, but without so much as a comma between, I would have to add my exquisite treasure of friends and family. What are you collecting?[192]

PEGGY BENSON

FRIDAY

WATCH FOR THE FIREWORKS

The Mighty One blesses you.
He gives you blessings from the highest heavens.
He gives you blessings from the deepest oceans.
He blesses you with children and with a mother's milk.

GENESIS 49:25 NIRV

Our support group has met monthly in a church across from Disneyland. During the summer months, the 9:30 P.M. fireworks over Disneyland always interrupt our meetings. I'd usually get irritated and annoyed until one evening a couple from Iowa joined us. As soon as the fireworks started, they sat up, eyes twinkling. "Oh, the fireworks!" they exclaimed. There was wonder in their faces. They were excited and suddenly animated.

Think of everything you normally take for granted. Make a list of the most ordinary, tedious things that happen every day over and over in your life. Now imagine a homeless man or woman coming to live with you for a day. What do you think they would say about the linens and soft blankets?

We may as well get enthused and infect everyone we meet with God's amazing love and joy in living. Let the fireworks begin![193]

BARBARA JOHNSON

WEEKEND

CREATIVE ENCOURAGEMENT

The LORD and King has taught me what to say.
He has taught me how to help those who are tired.
He wakes me up every morning.
He makes me want to listen like a good student.

ISAIAH 50:4 NIRV

I admire people who know how to encourage others by what they say and do. But even if you weren't born with the gift of encouragement, you still can do it. God is more than willing to teach you. The all-time great Encourager says he will give you his words to sustain those around you. He even wants to show you, first thing in the morning, those who may need an encouraging word.

What does God require of you, his student? "Listen like one being taught." Cooperate with the Lord when he nudges you to say a kind word. Encouraging others costs no more than a bit of time and effort. Yet who can put a price on its value?

JONI EARECKSON TADA

Thank you, Lord, for instructing me to be an encourager.
Teach me to listen attentively to you and then
to eagerly step out to offer whatever creative form
of encouragement occurs to me.[194] Amen.

MONDAY

❁

A PERFECT FRIENDSHIP

Some friends play at friendship
  but a true friend sticks closer than one's nearest kin.

PROVERBS 18:24 NRSV

What a joy for two people when each is a shady covering for the other—a place to rest when the sun is too hot or the wind too biting. Friendship is good for your health, too—even your cardiovascular and immune systems. We need good friends even if we have wonderful spouses. We need other people with whom we can laugh and cry.

When we're all anchored in the same harbor, we're able to help each other patch the holes in our boats. If a friend has hurt my feelings, I find it hard to be honest about that. But sometimes speaking the truth about a hurt is very important. When we can walk through that field with a few thorns in the grass and make it to the other side, our friendships will be stronger, and our joy will be real.[195]

Pray often for the true friends in your life, and ask God to help you be a true friend to those who care for you.

SHEILA WALSH

TUESDAY

PEOPLE ARE LIKE PLANTS

Perfume and incense bring joy to the heart,
and the pleasantness of one's friend springs
from his earnest counsel.

PROVERBS 27:9

Like people, plants are born with personality. The difference, I think, is that in his plan for people, God added humor!

Some plants feed upon a seed beneath the earth. Others push the seed case forth—some with methodical care, others with reckless abandonment.

I am often gently nourished by a friend whose quiet company provides wisdom and comfort for my spirit. I am sometimes coquettishly coaxed from my comfortable environment and persistently urged through the crusty surface soil by friends. But on occasion, I have been catapulted from my warm bed to worlds beyond my experience by the likes of my professional colleagues or family members.

We nurture and are nourished by our friends in different ways. In his plan for friends, I think God often paints way outside the lines. The color may not rival that of the flower garden, but the comedy is superb![196]

JOY MacKENZIE

WEDNESDAY

❖

A GOOD SOLDIER

Endure hardship with us like a good soldier of Christ Jesus. No one serving as a soldier gets involved in civilian affairs—he wants to please his commanding officer.

2 TIMOTHY 2:3–4

The soldier who is called to the front lines is stimulated at the chance to prove his skills. The officer who is given a position of higher responsibility is roused by the rugged demands of his task.

You and I are soldiers in the same way. If you are tempted to slack off from praying, but instead you remain faithful, your faith develops perseverance. If you are tempted to feel sorry for yourself, but instead you start thinking of the needs of others, your character becomes refined. The result? Greater faith and a closer fellowship with the Savior.

And that is where the joy comes in!

It's going to happen to you scores of times today. God may test you. The devil may tempt you. And you may backslide or advance. You can either fudge the truth or stand firm on the facts. When it happens, consider each test and temptation an opportunity to be seized, a chance to prove your faith. Your goal? A closer friendship with God.[197]

JONI EARECKSON TADA

THURSDAY

A JOYFUL ADVENTURE
OF THE HEART

I press on toward the goal to win the prize for which God has called me heavenward in Christ Jesus.

PHILIPPIANS 3:14

I'm all for nostalgia, but it's hard to be nostalgic when you can't remember anything. I'm moving on, anticipating where I'm heading, open to today's answers to today's problems.

Some people pause to reminisce and then get stuck there. Nowadays I may be slowing down, but I am definitely not settling back. I keep trying. And if at first I do succeed, I'll try not to look astonished.

How will the Lord use your life? Is there one thing you can do to make life better for someone else? Can you warm the home of an elderly friend? Chill out so a teenager can open up to your love? Knock on the door of a lonely single mom? Invite a seven-year-old for lemonade? The possibilities are endless. God expects us to use our brains and figure out what we can do to make a difference. Find out where he's working and join his crew.[198] You'll find yourself on a joyful adventure of the heart.

BARBARA JOHNSON

FRIDAY

ABOVE THE CLOUDS

I also pray that your mind might see more clearly.
Then you will know the hope God has chosen
you to receive.

EPHESIANS 1:18 NIRV

O n the plane, I was very much aware of the rain pound-
ing against my window. I closed my eyes, thinking it
would be a miracle if I got through this day. I felt myself sinking deeper and deeper into hopelessness.

Suddenly, the sun shone so brightly that my eyes hurt from
the change. Above the clouds I saw a crystal blue backdrop and
a mixture of pink and purple hues outlining the sky in a most
perfect way. Before I could take it all in, the Lord spoke inside
of my spirit: *What you see now is what I see. You witnessed something*
totally different only moments ago. Never would you have believed that
right above those clouds is what looks like paradise. I will take you
through and past the storms. Things aren't what they seem.

I felt a weight lift as the Lord humbled my heart and drew
me close. He gave me that touch, that perspective I so badly
needed.[199] Seeing as he sees always brings joy.

KATHY TROCCOLI

WEEKEND

❋

RIDING LESSONS

*Physical training is of some value, but godliness
has value for all things, holding promise for both
the present life and the life to come.*

1 TIMOTHY 4:8

An unbridled, untrained horse lacks the restraints that
guide and direct. The bit, martingale, tie-down, spur,
and crop appear at first to the horse as irritants and hardships.
But such inconvenience and suffering school the horse to listen to the rider's commands. How hard it would be for an
animal, without the aid of his master and his crop, to train
himself up in the way he should go. What's more, the horse
would be useless in the ring, without a hope of ever winning
honors for his master.

It's the same for humans. As someone has said, freedom is
not the right to do what we want to do; it is the power to do
what we ought. Hardship is our bit and bridle. What's more,
our Master is an expert with the reins and the crop. We are
never more ourselves, never more spiritually free, than when
we take joy in bending our wills to God's will.[200]

JONI EARECKSON TADA

*Heavenly Father, I pray as Jesus did, "Not my will, but your
will be done." Guide me in the way you want me to go. Amen.*

MONDAY

WILLING TO KNOW OURSELVES

Know that the LORD is God.
It is he who made us, and we are his;
we are his people, the sheep of his pasture.

PSALM 100:3

If we are to find the courage to live an honest life before God, facing our fears and walking with *open* hands rather than hands that are grasping for control, we need to look at ourselves as we really are, rather than as we wish we were. In *Our Many Selves,* Elizabeth O'Connor observed, "We are only able to grow in our relationship with God to the extent that we are willing to know ourselves."

What I know is this: When I was supposedly at the best place in my life, I was totally miserable. I was on TV; I was a writer and singer, doing all the things I love to do—but I was lost. I look back on that time in utter amazement at the grace of God that burst through my pathetic attempts to feel good about myself. He longed to show me his love, to teach me that life is not just about me being "happy." It's much bigger than that; it's much better than that.[201]

SHEILA WALSH

TUESDAY

NOT ALL BEAUTIFUL THINGS
ARE GOOD

*Put all things to the test: keep what is good and avoid
every kind of evil.*

1 THESSALONIANS 5:21—22 GNT

The oleander bush thrives in the California climate, and
often blooms bright and colorful along the freeways.
Yes, oleanders are lovely, but they're deadly. Because the
leaves and blossoms are highly toxic, many pet lovers have
uprooted oleander bushes from their backyards. I once enter-
tained the idea of picking oleander flowers to use in a table
centerpiece but decided that I didn't relish the idea of placing
something poisonous on the dinner table.

Like oleanders, some ideas are beautiful but, oh, so deadly.
Bad thoughts never enter your mind, telling you, *I want to
ruin your peace of mind; I want to rob you of joy.* No, harmful
thoughts always disguise themselves as pleasant things to
ponder. But beware. So-called beautiful thoughts are like a
bouquet of oleanders on your dining-room table. They may
be attractive to look at, but they don't belong close to you.
Never learn to accept the idea of putting something poisonous
in front of you.[202]

JONI EARECKSON TADA

WEDNESDAY

✶

TIME ALONE WITH HIM

[Pray] that we may lead a tranquil and quiet life in all godliness and dignity.

1 TIMOTHY 2:2 NASB

The joy and pleasure of speaking with the Lord is far superior to anything life on this earth affords. Through prayer I become centered and serene. When it's quiet and still, I sense the Lord comes near as I enter his presence.

I experience a silent symmetry when I'm alone with him that makes me calm. It strengthens me for the task at hand. In a culture where we all but worship activity and accomplishment, we can so easily miss time alone with him.

Remember what he said to Martha, who was such a little busy beaver, living, I guess, a loud and active life. He said, "Martha, slow down. Look at Mary. She's sitting here calmly talking to me. That's the better thing to do."

When you're tempted to run around and not stop, let me challenge you. Choose the better part. Be with your friends, relax a little, and most necessarily, be the Savior for a while.[203]

LUCI SWINDOLL

THURSDAY

HE IS DELIGHTED ABOUT YOU

The LORD declares, "Here is my servant, whom I uphold, my chosen one in whom I delight."

ISAIAH 42:1

Have you ever "taken delight" in someone? Maybe you've burst into laughter over an infant's first smile. Perhaps you've beamed with pride as a dear one graduates from college with honors. Or maybe you've felt the delicious warmth of a loved one's gaze.

To take delight in someone close means to relish in his achievements. To be jubilant in her triumphs. To be captivated with his beauty and to find pleasure in the adoration and love given in return. And praise God, this is the way he feels about you!

When you obey, for instance, God doesn't merely observe from a distance and nod approvingly. He is not dispassionate about your obedience. He is delighted!

How it must give Jesus joy when we choose to obey. How it must delight him when he sees our face and hears our voice in praise. And just in case you still think God isn't emotional toward you, consider the words of Isaiah 62:5: "As a bridegroom rejoices over his bride, so will your God rejoice over you."[204]

JONI EARECKSON TADA

FRIDAY

FRESH-START JOY

Let them thank the LORD for his steadfast love,
for his wonderful works to humankind.

PSALM 107:8 NRSV

Each day that we live is a gift from God. Maybe that's why *today* is called "the present"! To unwrap this gift of everyday life, learn to make *gratitude* your *attitude*. Start focusing on all the blessings God has infused into your life, instead of the problems you encounter.

All of us have plenty of opportunities to worry, but we must remember that worry never accomplishes anything—except to make us miserable. Instead of fretting about what might happen, we need to realize that God puts a veil across our way so we don't know what's ahead of us. He hides the future so that we will learn to trust him for our daily existence just as simply as do the lilies of the field. Jesus told us the lilies don't worry about tomorrow—and neither should we.

Try waking up tomorrow with a grateful heart that's thankful for another day to serve God and his kingdom. That attitude is fresh-start joy.[205]

BARBARA JOHNSON

WEEKEND

CREATE JOY

Encourage the timid, help the weak,
be patient with everyone.... Always try to be kind
to each other and to everyone else.... Be joyful always.

1 THESSALONIANS 5:14–16

Encouragement is one of God's most joyous art forms. He supplies us with the raw materials and invites us to create, build, and shape his hope in the lives of those around us.

Some people combine a helping hand with a word of praise and produce a grateful heart. Others, by mixing laughter and love, are able to paint new sparkle in dulling eyes. Belief and support build self-esteem. Persistent prayer composes a song of hope; and tenderness and warm embraces fashion a friend.

However we combine the elements of encouragement, one thing we're sure to create is joy—for others, for ourselves, and for our Lord.[206]

SUSAN LENKES

Heavenly Father, I want to be a creator of joy everywhere I go.
Open my eyes to the many blessings you have given me, and
use me to help others see the ways you have blessed them. Give
me the right words at the right time to encourage, build up,
praise, support, and comfort the people in my world. Amen.

MONDAY

✦

REAL FRIENDSHIP

Rejoice with them that do rejoice, and weep with them that weep.

ROMANS 12:15 KJV

O ne of the deepest callings of friendship is to weep with those who weep. There are seasons in all of our lives when the wind blows cold and we feel fragile and exposed, when we wrap each other up in a blanket of love and friendship and stay right there until the buds begin to show again.

We were formed for relationship, but we are filled in Christ. Our deepest needs for intimacy will be met only in the "friend who sticks closer than a brother" (Proverbs 18:24).[207] God, who is that friend, shows us what true friendship is all about—being there for each other. When you are filled up with him, you can weep with a friend who weeps and be there for her in her darkest hour. You will also be able to point her to Jesus, so her joy can be restored.

SHEILA WALSH

TUESDAY

THE BEAUTY OF FREEDOM

The Lord is the Holy Spirit. And where
the Spirit of the Lord is, freedom is also there.

2 CORINTHIANS 3:17 NIRV

J esus never said to his disciples, "Obey my rules." Instead,
he told his followers, "Obey me." Because he didn't leave
us with a long list of "Thou shalt nots," we have freedom.

Jesus stripped the fear and intimidation away from obedience when he wrapped his life around his Word. What
liberty! The Lord made obedience something that you would
desire to do because he gave his life that you might be free.
What a brilliant motivation for us to trust and obey!

Sometimes I wish that God would give me less freedom
and force me to do the right thing—make me obey. It would
be easier that way. This "freedom stuff" carries with it a heavy
weight of responsibility. I am required to discern between
white and black, light and dark, good and evil. I am required
to make choices. I am required to be free.

But that's the beauty of the freedom of the Lord. And it is
his love that makes me want to obey.[208]

JONI EARECKSON TADA

WEDNESDAY

❁

A PARENT'S PRAYER

You are my fortress,
my refuge in times of trouble.

PSALM 59:16

A parent's life is hard. Just as you're sighing with relief after getting the kids through diapers, daycare, and diplomas, along comes a genuine disaster that makes you long for the days when your biggest dilemma was preparing enough formula or getting all the diapers laundered. When these life storms crash over us, the only thing we can do is love—love God and love our children, and turn them over to the Lord. Proverbs 10:12 reminds us, "Love covers over all wrongs," and that's true for all of God's children.

How wonderful for us hurting parents that we don't have to endure life's tragedies alone. Our loving heavenly Father is with us when our children break our hearts. Clinging to God's Word, we keep breathing and keep believing. As the psalmist wrote, "My comfort in my suffering is this: Your promise preserves my life" (Psalm 119:50).[209]

BARBARA JOHNSON

THURSDAY

❈

PIT STOPS

Banish anxiety from your heart
and cast off the troubles of your body.

ECCLESIASTES 11:10

If you're speeding down the freeway, the police might pull you over. But no one ever makes you take pit stops. You have to choose them. It's the same with life. Emergencies force us to stop, but pit stops of joy are events we must plan for and savor.

It's good to let go and laugh when life is weighing you down. It won't change any of the circumstances in which you find yourself, but when you can laugh at the antics of others, it helps lighten the load.

Does something come to mind for you? It could be an old black-and-white episode of Andy Griffith or the time Lucy and Ethel worked in the chocolate factory. It might be a video of family and friends that makes you laugh when you watch it. Or maybe it's an old tearjerker movie with a happy ending. Pop in the tape, stock up on the snacks, and put your feet up. Treat yourself to a few laughs and a much-needed pit stop.[210]

SHEILA WALSH

FRIDAY

NO PARKING

*Not that I have already obtained all this, or have
already been made perfect, but I press on to take hold
of that for which Christ Jesus took hold of me.*

PHILIPPIANS 3:12

As believers in God, there are places where we should
definitely not, under any circumstances, even *think* of
parking.

Do not park by life's defeats. Where has life gotten you down?
Don't park there! Move on.

Do not park at anger. Storing up hostility will only boomerang
on you in the long run.

Do not park at escape. There is no good time for quitting.
Don't give up—get going!

Do not park at discouragement. Optimism actually promotes
physical as well as emotional healing.

Do not park at worry. Think on what is right and true and
lovely (Philippians 4:8). Who knows what possibilities are just
around the corner?

Do not park at guilt. Move on by receiving Jesus as your
Savior, accepting God's forgiveness, and freely forgiving
others. Put the past behind you. Begin again.[211]

BARBARA JOHNSON

WEEKEND

IT'S TIME TO CELEBRATE!

The LORD says,
"I have loved you with an everlasting love;
* I have drawn you with loving-kindness.*
I will build you up again."

JEREMIAH 31:3–4

If you've messed up and tried to come home, only to find yourself rejected, I ache for you. I ache to think of the millions of people who have fallen through the arms of the body of Christ, wounded and unable to cry out for help for fear that they would be ostracized. But let me tell you this: There is a party going on in your honor, and it's being thrown by God Almighty. So get down on your knees and say, "Thank you." Buy yourself a party hat and a big cake, and invite some other lost souls to celebrate God's joy at your homecoming. Open your heart and open your ears, and you will hear, "My son! My daughter! Come on in to the party!"[212]

SHEILA WALSH

Heavenly Father, you know where I've been
and what I've done. You know all about me and
love me anyway. This is more than I can take in,
but I believe it because your Word tells me so. Amen.

MONDAY

THE ENEMY CALLED REGRET

Godly sorrow brings repentance that leads to salvation and leaves no regret.

2 CORINTHIANS 7:10

Ever wish you could start over? Probably all of us have longed for another chance in some area of our lives. We wouldn't necessarily have done things differently, just done more or perhaps done less of one thing or another.

The truth is, we can't go backward, only forward into uncharted territory. To sit still in our sorrow would lead to misery. Although regret that leads to change is a dear friend, regret that leads to shame is a treacherous enemy.

There is no guarantee that if we had done a part of our lives differently, things would have ended up any differently. We have to trust the God of the universe, who directs the outcome of all things, that he will do that which ultimately needs to be done.

Many things are out of our control, but they are never out of his. So the next time you and I need something to lean on, let's make it the Lord.[213] Let's take joy in change and abandon regret.

PATSY CLAIRMONT

TUESDAY

OBEY WITH RECKLESS JOY

By dying to what once bound us, we have been released from the law so that we serve in the new way of the Spirit, and not in the old way of the written code.

ROMANS 7:6

The longer the written code, the more oppressive the pressure is to obey. A list of dos and don'ts seems tiring. Obtrusive. Burdensome. The more you concentrate on them, the more tempted you are to break the law.

Thank God, we have been released to serve the Lord in the new way of the Spirit and not in the old way of the written code. We serve Jesus; we don't serve a list of rules. This is exactly why we should stop using words like *victory* and *defeat* to describe our obedience. We are never defeated by this or that sin. Rather, we are obedient or disobedient to the Lord.

If you see obedience as merely a duty, it will quickly become a burden. The letter of the word has no saving or sanctifying power—and human will, no matter how strenuous, cannot give that power. So look to Jesus and obey him with glad, reckless joy.[214]

JONI EARECKSON TADA

WEDNESDAY

✦

SCATTER JOY

How beautiful on the mountains
  are the feet of those who bring good news,
who proclaim peace,
  who bring good tidings,
  who proclaim salvation,
who say to Zion,
  "Your God reigns!"

ISAIAH 52:7

I believe in having fun, because I know that she who laughs, lasts. Whatever you do, whether it's jumping from airplanes, visiting the sick, surfing the Net, taking care of widows, or goofing off, do it well, and never lose your ability to scatter joy. Tuck some in the pocket of the stranger next to you at the grocery store. Leave funny messages in your teenagers' cars or on their email. Wake your spouse up with the scent of roses or honeysuckle. And never, ever forget to smile.

Smiles are like two-for-one coupons. Each time you let them spread across your lips, they light up the face and heart of someone else. Sooner or later a smile will come back around to you just when you need it most. And it is something anyone—everyone—can do well. [215]

BARBARA JOHNSON

THURSDAY

COURAGE TO CRY

You know how troubled I am;
*   you have kept a record of my tears.*
Aren't they listed in your book?

PSALM 56:8 GNT

Years ago when I was in the hospital, I noticed something peculiar. Even though there was so much pain in the lives of my roommates, even though I knew they were hurting, no one cried. Sometimes I would lie awake in the middle of the night, wanting so much to cry, but afraid to. I was afraid I would wake up my roommates and maybe, just maybe, they would make fun of me the next day at physical therapy. So I kept my tears to myself.

After I got out of the hospital, I learned about David, the warrior-king who cried, and big, burly Peter who wept bitterly when he recognized his sin. I read about Jesus who offered prayers and petitions "with loud cries and tears."

Learning about these people in Scripture gave me the courage to cry. No longer were tears an embarrassment, a mark of weakness or shame. Out of our grief, God will bring the reward of joy that will last forever.[216]

JONI EARECKSON TADA

FRIDAY

THE JOY OF BEING A CHILD

The LORD said,
"I have loved you with a love that lasts forever.
I have kept on loving you with faithful love."

JEREMIAH 31:3 NIRV

My baby boy has no sense of what's appropriate on the noise-making front. On the first Sunday we took him to church, we opted to sit in the back row. As the sermon started, Christian was cuddled up in my arms, deep in sleep, or so I thought. Suddenly, Christian burst into a baby version of "Moon River" at a decibel level that could have burst a dog's eardrums. I jumped up and hurried out, whispering "Shh!" vainly in his ear. That only seemed to encourage him, and he moved into verse two, grinning from ear to ear. By the time we were outside, I was laughing so hard I could barely walk or breathe.

When children are secure, they feel free to be who they really are. That's how you and I can live, too. God is the only One who knows everything about us, and he loves you. What a gift in a world where there is so much uncertainty![217]

SHEILA WALSH

WEEKEND

❋

A TRANSPARENT LIFE

Be very careful, then, how you live—not as unwise but as wise.

EPHESIANS 5:15

I am humbled when I read how God wants me to treat others, and I know I need to grow in my heart's capacity to love in a way that puts others above myself. What if you and I were videotaped and then the video were played back in front of our church? Would we talk and act differently?

The truth is that God is watching. Not with a gigantic stick in one hand and a check-off list in the other, but with eyes that see to our very core—eyes desiring that we live in the riches of his grace so that we may be able to eat of the good fruit that comes from a life rooted in love.[218] A transparent life is a joyful life.

KATHY TROCCOLI

Heavenly Father, I am humbled when I realize
that you know my every thought, word, and action.
Help me walk in a way that is pleasing to you and
that will represent you well to others. Amen.

MONDAY

❖

LEAP FOR JOY

Jesus said, "Rejoice in that day and leap for joy,
because great is your reward in heaven."

I t's a word you read often in Scripture. Mary rejoiced when
the angel announced she would bear the Savior. Angels
rejoiced in the sky over Bethlehem. People rejoiced to see
lame men walk and deaf men hear. The women rejoiced as
they raced from the empty tomb. Even the apostle Paul commanded, "Be joyful always."

But Jesus takes it a step farther when he exclaims, "Leap
for joy!" This is no sedate and dispassionate command. You
can't be dignified and demure when you're exclaiming. In fact,
scholars note that the word *rejoice* is best communicated with
a jump-up-and-down, clenched fist, throw-your-head-back,
and yell-out-loud, "Oh, joy!"

The people in Scripture were not plaster-of-paris saints
who uttered their astonishment in less-than-amazing tones.
When they exclaimed surprise or excitement, you'd better
believe they were bursting with joy. So when you read Scripture,
never read the word *rejoice* without a smile. Remember, God's
Word is alive and active, full of feeling and brimming with
heartfelt emotion.[219]

JONI EARECKSON TADA

TUESDAY

AWAKE IN THE NIGHT

As I lie on my bed I remember you.
I think of you all night long.

PSALM 63:6 NIRV

I resent the need for sleep. I can't remember a time in my life when the call to sleep was appealing. But two thoughts comfort me. When Scripture states that God watches over us and will not slumber, I'm thrilled to realize that should I wake up in the night, he's awake, too. I hate being the only one awake in the night. Some of my best times with him have occurred during the wee hours of the morning when no one else is alert. I've settled enormous issues during some of those nocturnal chats. Other times I've just felt comforted by his presence. Sometimes there's no talk at all. I just know he's there.

The other comfort is that because God does not sleep, and because Scripture says in heaven I shall be like him, the day is coming when I, too, won't have to sleep! That heavenly prospect floods me with joy, as well as anticipation—what a reward for going to bed on earth![220]

MARILYN MEBERG

WEDNESDAY

✤

WHAT ARE YOU THANKFUL FOR?

Devote yourselves to prayer, being watchful and thankful.

I don't know about you, but I don't want to live my life in the *past* lane. I want to find a zillion things to be thankful for today. One little girl was overjoyed one Thanksgiving Day because broccoli *wasn't* on the table! When God does make broccoli part of the menu, I've learned it's only because he has a greater good in mind.

What are you thankful for right at this moment? Start today by being grateful for the tiniest things: water to drink, a moment to rest, the color of a flower or sunset or bird. A piece of bread. A song on the radio. Keep looking for sights, smells, sounds, that make you feel pleasure. Write them down.

Let's decide to be thankful and encourage one another to cultivate grateful hearts. God is thankful for *you*. He gave his Son to reclaim your life. He invites you into the joy of salvation. That's an awful lot to be thankful for right there.[221]

BARBARA JOHNSON

THURSDAY

❋

INTO HIS HANDS

My times are in your hands.

PSALM 31:15

L ife is very lonely when we sit in our private dungeons of despair, whistling a song that, if we would only open up our lungs and let rip, we would hear it echoed from prison walls all around us.

In Christ we have the perfect pattern of One who told the truth, no matter the cost; who faced his fear, no matter the pain; and who found peace in the will of his Father. "Jesus called out with a loud voice, 'Father, into your hands I commit my spirit.' When he had said this, he breathed his last" (Luke 23:46). Jesus' words echoed the psalmist's. David was a man who had struggled and failed and struggled again. "Into your hands I commit my spirit; redeem me, O LORD, the God of truth" (Psalm 31:5).

Those seem to be the words of the greatest lovers of God.

Into your hands.

Into your hands.

Into your hands. [222]

It is the place of ultimate joy—in his hands.

SHEILA WALSH

FRIDAY

FAMILY PHOTOS

*Jesus said, "Are not two sparrows sold for a penny?
Yet not one of them will fall to the ground apart from
the will of your Father. And even the very hairs of your
head are all numbered. So don't be afraid; you are
worth more than many sparrows."*

MATTHEW 10:29–31

Wandering through an antique shop, my husband and I spotted a photo album on a table. Interested, we peeked inside only to find a family peering back at us.

We both felt sad, wondering who would throw away his or her history (a few family members maybe, but the whole clan)? How does one toss out a picture without guilt? A person's likeness is so personal that it seems like a violation to discard them. After all, what if these individuals have rejection issues? And who would purpose to buy more relatives?

Ever feel like your identity is lost in a world full of people? We have a God whose heart is expansive enough to hold us all and yet who's so intently focused on each of us that he knows our rising up and our sitting down. Our faces are no surprise to the Lord. He takes joy in us, and our identities are engraved in the palms of his hands.[223]

PATSY CLAIRMONT

WEEKEND

PUT ON A NEW RECORD

Do not use harmful words, but only helpful words,
the kind that build up and provide what is needed,
so that what you say will do good to those who hear you.

EPHESIANS 4:29 GNT

True love demands honesty, taking risks with one another and enduring some difficult moments because we want a real relationship.

A friend of mine recently told me he now only talks to his mother by e-mail because it makes her more bearable. I asked him if he had ever discussed with her the difficulty they had communicating. He looked at me as if I had suggested he stick his hand in a blender. "You've got to be kidding," he said. "Talk to my mother? That's like trying to bargain with a scorpion!"

Often family members behave in set patterns simply because that's what we expect each other to do. It's a dance that has developed over the years between us. We need to take a fresh look. Put on a new record. Say "thank you." Send flowers. Write a note. Take a good look. Move a little closer.[224]

SHEILA WALSH

Heavenly Father, help my family members
and me to establish new and healthy patterns
of relating to one another. Amen.

MONDAY

SET APART

You created my inmost being;
*   you knit me together in my mother's womb....*
All the days ordained for me
*   were written in your book before one of them came to be.*

PSALM 139:13, 16

We want and need to know who we are. Of course, for the believer, it need not be a puzzle.

Specific attention, thought, and planning about me took place before God actually formed me in the womb. That implies that I am much more than the result of a cozy encounter between my parents nine months before I was born. No matter the circumstances surrounding my conception, I am a planned event. Not only am I a planned event, I was "set apart." I have a specific task to do for God.

We all have a specific task to do for God, and it was planned in his head before we were ever formed in the womb. That is an incredible truth!

Not only is my identity and calling known, but also he considers me unique and set apart, and he calls me his own. May we sink into that cushion of joyful peace and never forget "whose we be."[225]

MARILYN MEBERG

TUESDAY

PRECIOUS PROMISES

Restore to me the joy of your salvation.

PSALM 51:12

Two years after becoming single, I frequently found myself in tears at suppertime. My toddlers seemed to be tired by then, scrapping with each other, whining, hanging onto me.

This is when Daddy is supposed to appear at the door, and both children run to their hero. Dad's arrival gives Mom a few minutes of peace while she prepares the evening meal, and later, she has someone with whom to share and commiserate.

But no one comes while I'm preparing supper. And after a year of grieving for the loss of mate, companion, and father of my children, I knew I had to do something to survive the suppertime slump. I remembered some promises about joy that I'd cut out and stuck in a drawer years before. "You will grieve, but your grief will turn to joy…and no one will take away your joy" (John 16:20, 22). Though yellowed, wrinkled, and stained with an ancient cake batter, my promises were more precious than gold![226]

SUE RICHARDS

WEDNESDAY

❋

LEAD OTHERS TO GOD'S EMBRACE

We are God's workmanship, created in Christ Jesus to do good works, which God prepared in advance for us to do.

EPHESIANS 2:10

I hope to be a woman who is real and compassionate and who might draw people to nestle within God's embrace.

Any one of us can do that. We may never win any great awards, but each of us has an arm with which to hold another person. Each of us can pull another shoulder under ours, invite someone in need to nestle next to our heart. We can give a pat on the back, a simple compliment, a kiss on the cheek, a thumbs-up sign. We can smile at a stranger, say hello when it's least expected, send a card of congratulations, take flowers to a sick neighbor, make a casserole for a new mother.

Let's take the things that set us apart, that make us different, that cause us to disagree, and make them an occasion to compliment each other and be thankful for each other. Let us be big enough to be smaller than our neighbor, spouse, friends, and strangers. Every day.[227] It'll make your heart glad.

BARBARA JOHNSON

THURSDAY

WHAT JOY LOOKS LIKE

*The heavens proclaim his righteousness,
and all the peoples see his glory.*

PSALM 97:6

Early Christmas morning! Waking up in a cold bedroom, frost on the windowpanes, snow draping the trees outside my window. Wrapping up in warm dressing gowns and slippers. Creeping down the stairs barely able to contain the excitement. Opening the living-room door…a wonderland, a transformation overnight from the ordinary to every unspoken wish laid out in gold and red and green packages. Tangerines wrapped in silver paper. The aroma of turkey filling every room.

I wonder why our vision becomes impaired with the turning of calendar pages. We have forgotten what joy looks like. We were made for joy, but we have forgotten what it smells like. We've forgotten how it sounds.

Before you go to bed tonight, do one thing that will bring back a little joy from childhood. Have some cookies and milk or throw a duckie in your bath. Buy a children's book and curl up by the fire and read. Welcome to … joy![228]

SHEILA WALSH

FRIDAY

WHY ME, LORD?

God disciplines us for our good, that we may share in his holiness.

HEBREWS 12:10

Some days everything seems to go wrong. The plumbing decides to back up; the furnace dies; the car has a flat; and the stomach flu topples the whole household.

Then there are the more serious events that enter our lives—seemingly without reason. The ones that slice at our very roots: a lost job, an extended illness, an accident, money trouble.

Do you ever wonder about the calamities that meet us head-on in everyday life? Do you ever ask, as I do, *Why me, Lord?* Is there a reason behind these catastrophies?

What a difference it makes if we face the calamities in our lives with an attitude of joy. Not a fake, pasted-on joy—but a joy that comes from knowing that God is bringing us closer to sharing in his holiness—through discipline.

So the next time those rough winds sweep through—let's rejoice! It won't be long until we can lift our hearts and laugh in his sunshine … in his holiness.[229]

DIANE HEAD

WEEKEND

❂

PURE TO THE CORE

*He will bring to light what is hidden in darkness
and will expose the motives of men's hearts.
At that time each will receive his praise from God.*

1 CORINTHIANS 4:5

*G*od will expose the motives of our hearts. This verse hits me
at my core, and it is my core the Lord is concerned about.

Most of us look pretty good on the outside. Our works are
noble. Our lives seem to be in decent order. But the Lord looks
beyond all that and into our hearts. He sees exactly from what
source our waters flow. Are we drinking from the river of life
or from streams that originate in our own will? I pray we will
desire pure hearts and pure motives, that we will let his light
pierce through the darkness to expose all that is not of
him.[230] Only then can we truly know the joy of the Lord.

KATHY TROCCOLI

*Heavenly Father, it is both unnerving and comforting
to know that you know my heart. Unnerving to realize
you see all the junk. Comforting that you know me and
still you love me. Bring to light all that is not of you,
so it can be washed clean by Jesus' blood. Amen.*

MONDAY

BECOME A JOY COLLECTOR

It is good to be able to enjoy the pleasant light of day.
Be grateful for every year you live.

ECCLESIASTES 11:7–8 GNT

God can use you even when you're living between estrogen and death. Age on, girls—the best is yet to be! Remember that each day is like a suitcase—every person gets the same size, but some people figure out how to pack more into theirs.

It's easy to deny yourself many of life's simple pleasures because you want to be practical. Forget about practical and decide instead to become a joy collector. Always be on the lookout for gifts without ribbons. God's gifts come tagged with a note: "Life can be wonderful. Do your best not to miss it!" Enjoy what is, before it isn't anymore.

Don't be like the woman who described herself as passive and bored, a "mush melon living in a middle-aged frame." Instead be zany and giddy. Dare to slip on a pair of bunny slippers once in a while! Surprise yourself! Enjoy the little things, because one day you'll look back and realize they were the big things.[231]

BARBARA JOHNSON

TUESDAY

NOTHING ELSE WILL DO

We who are still alive and are left will be caught up together with them in the clouds to meet the Lord in the air. And so we will ever be with the Lord forever. Therefore encourage each other with these words.

1 THESSALONIANS 4:17–18

What is our future? Paul wrote that God has placed within our hearts a longing for what is not available down here, so that nothing else will do: Second Corinthians 5:5 in Eugene Peterson's *The Message* says, "We've been given a glimpse of the real thing, our true home, our resurrection bodies! The Spirit of God whets our appetite by giving us a taste of what's ahead. He puts a little of heaven in our hearts so that we'll never settle for less."

What we truly long for is just not available this side of heaven. For me, this is strangely good news. It's like that annoying missing piece of a puzzle. As I continue to reinterpret the purpose of my life, gaining an understanding of this truth has been life-changing for me. I can stop spending every waking moment searching under the same cushions and through the same drawers for a puzzle piece that is not in my possession. I can give myself to something infinitely more worthwhile.[232]

SHEILA WALSH

WEDNESDAY

❖

A TIME TO PLAY

Jesus said, "What I'm about to tell you is true.
Anyone who will not receive God's kingdom like a little
child will never enter it." Then he took the children in
his arms. He put his hands on them and blessed them.

MARK 10:15–16 NIRV

I love playful people! People who aren't too sophisticated
or too proper to engage in zany antics draw me like a two-
year-old to mud.

Sometimes I think we responsible adults assume that being
playful might be interpreted as being childish, maybe even
silly. Admittedly, nothing is more tragic than an adult who fails
to gain the maturity and wisdom necessary to live a productive life. But equally tragic are adults who forget how to vent
their play instincts. The mature person is able to recognize the
distinction between the two worlds and choose which world
is appropriate for the moment.

Jesus said it's impossible to enter the kingdom unless we
become as little children. He reminds us of how preferable it
is at times to be childlike.[233]

Allow yourself to be a playful child at times. God won't
fault you for your display of spontaneity and joy.

MARILYN MEBERG

THURSDAY

NEVER FORGOTTEN

The LORD declares,
"Can a mother forget the baby at her breast
and have no compassion on the child she has borne?
Though she may forget,
I will not forget you!"

ISAIAH 49:15

A friend asked me to be the surprise guest for the employees at their annual Christmas dinner. I agreed. But I didn't write it down. The day of the event, I kept feeling this annoying tug that said, *You're supposed to do something today*. But I couldn't think of what it was.

On Christmas Day, someone asked me how the surprise appearance had worked out. *Oh, no!* My heart was sick.

Wouldn't it be horrible if Jesus were so busy he couldn't remember what we talked to him about? Thank God we don't have to endure that kind of treatment from our Lord! God can be depended on. We disappoint loved ones. We inconvenience people we care about. But how wonderful, how beautiful, how comforting to know we have a God who is always near to console and cheer, just when we need him most.[234]

That's the joy of our salvation.

THELMA WELLS

FRIDAY

THE NOBLE SPOON

*In a large house there are articles not only of gold
and silver, but also of wood and clay; some are for
noble purposes and some for ignoble. If a man cleanses
himself from the latter, he will be an instrument
for noble purposes, made holy, useful to the Master
and prepared to do any good work.*

2 TIMOTHY 2:20—21

I was having lunch at a friend's home recently, a wise
Christian woman with discerning eyes. Before we ate, I
had to borrow one of her spoons and have her bend and twist
it in a contorted angle, so I could feed myself.

When lunch was over, I offered to have my husband
straighten it out, but she protested. "I want to keep this spoon
just the way it is. You can only use a spoon that's been bent. A
straight one won't do. A twisted tool in your hand can better
accomplish a task."

She's right. God can better accomplish his unique plan
when he bends us to suit his will. This makes us different from
most people (just like my spoon doesn't look like the rest of the
utensils in the kitchen drawer). Isn't it great to realize you are a
chosen vessel for God—perfectly suited for his joyous use?[235]

JONI EARECKSON TADA

WEEKEND

✦

MAKE PEACE WITH
THE TIMEPIECE

He will be the sure foundation for your times.

ISAIAH 33:6

I feel encased within a timepiece that can at times rob me of my peace. Left unto ourselves, some of us would race and others of us would rust. Either way, we would speed past or sleep through the joy. We need to make peace with the timepiece so we don't spend our time beating our heads against the clock.

Here are some tips. I'll try them if you will.

1. Don't cram every day so full that you can't enjoy the journey.

2. Don't under-plan and miss the thrill of a fruitful day.

3. Don't underestimate a nap, a rocking chair, or a good book.

4. Don't become a sloth.

5. Do offer your gratitude for the moments assigned to you.

6. Do celebrate even the passing of days.[236]

PATSY CLAIRMONT

*Heavenly Father, I resist the temptation to be
a slave to time. Help me to make the most of each day
and to live it in a way that pleases you. Amen.*

MONDAY

INCLUDING THE FORGOTTEN

*Jesus said, "When you give a banquet, invite the poor,
the crippled, the lame, the blind, and you will be
blessed. Although they cannot repay you, you will
be repaid at the resurrection of the righteous."*

LUKE 14:13–14

We rang the doorbell, and I laughed as I looked through the door's glass pane and saw four shaggy dogs running over each other to be first to the door. As we sat in our friends' study, eventually the dogs all found their places, flopping down.

"Do you make a habit of rescuing dogs from the pound?" I asked.

"Yes, I do," Karalyn answered. "Everyone wants a perfect animal, a new one that looks great with no faults or limitations, but I've found that the animals who have been all but tossed away have so much love to give."

Christ said that we shouldn't entertain those who can repay us, but rather those who have nothing to give. In every church across America, there are those who come lonely and leave lonely every Sunday. What a blessing it would be to them and to us if we really saw them and included them in our lives.[237] Think of the joy!

SHEILA WALSH

TUESDAY

ON MY FEET WALKING

We ourselves, who have the firstfruits of the Spirit,
groan inwardly as we wait eagerly for our adoption
as sons, the redemption of our bodies.
For in this hope we are saved.

ROMANS 8:23—24

When Ken and I were back in Maryland, my family showed home movies. There on the living-room wall, I saw myself at the age of sixteen. Later on Ken asked me how I felt as I watched myself walk. "There was a time I would have said, 'Aww, that's the way it used to be. I wish I could go back to that,'" I answered. "But now, thirty years later and having spent years sinking my heart and head into the Word of God, I can say, 'Oh, wow, this is the way it soon will be. I can look forward to having a body that works. And I'll do so much more than walk!'"

I am closer to this side of gaining my heavenly body than to the other side of losing my earthly body. The past is the past. The future is much more interesting to think about. Watching home movies fills me with joy to think of all I will gain back—and more![238]

JONI EARECKSON TADA

WEDNESDAY

❋

JOHNNY JUMP-UPS

He is like a tree that is planted near a stream of water.
It always bears its fruit at the right time.

PSALM 1:3 NIRV

One of my favorite early spring flowers is the Johnny Jump-Up. It is a first cousin to the pansy. They have sweet smiling faces, each with its own personality. Each morning, these happy faces of the small flowers look up at me as they settle their roots into the earth.

I smile back as I see in them the faces of my "jump-up" friends—people who have come into my life over the years at just the exact time I needed to see a friendly, smiling face. They are people who believe in me and let me know it in many ways. They are quick to send a note of encouragement, make a phone call, or surprise me with a birthday gift. What a tremendous rescue team![239]

Who are the Johnny Jump-Ups in your life? If you can't think of any, become someone else's Johnny Jump-Up. You'll soon find them popping up all around you.

PEGGY BENSON

THURSDAY

JESUS, THE PROMISE KEEPER

*Joshua said, "You know with all your heart
and soul that not one of all the good promises
the LORD your God gave you has failed.
Every promise has been fulfilled; not one has failed."*

JOSHUA 23:14

He stood out in a crowd—a tall, handsome black man from Jamaica with a big smile. I saw him shaking people's hands and heard each person tell him how encouraging his testimony was. As the crowd thinned, I wheeled up to him, leaned forward, and lifted my arm, a hint to let him know I wanted to shake hands. He smiled and leaned forward to extend his hand. Then a surprising thing happened: I realized he had no hands. This joyful Christian wore black fiberglass hands. We commented that even though we couldn't feel it, our "handshake" sure looked good!

He smiled broadly and said, "Sister, aren't you glad we have Jesus? We have his promises! Jesus and his promises—they are virtually one and the same." This disabled man from a poor country has staked his life on God's promises.

What promises anchor your faith? Can you say that not one of them has failed? You can if your anchor is Jesus.[240]

JONI EARECKSON TADA

FRIDAY

YOUNG AT HEART

Gray hair is a crown of splendor;
it is attained by a righteous life.

PROVERBS 16:31

A joyful heart will keep you young.

Television journalist Dan Rather once asked a 106-year-old man to disclose his secret of long life. The old man rocked back and forth in his chair before answering. Finally he replied, "Keep breathing."

Sure, growing older is stressful, but using your funny bone to subdue that kind of stress works wonders! When you hear snap, crackle, pop, and it isn't your cereal, don't panic. Laughter defuses insults, soothes aching muscles, and counteracts the humiliation of what is happening to your body and mind.

Gerontologist Ann E. Gerike says we can develop a new way of thinking about our physical limitations as we age. After a lifetime of straining to be "the perfect perky ideal," finally your breasts can relax. And that extra weight around the middle (hence the term "middle age"?)—it's just cuddlier body lines! So as birthdays come, don't think of yourself as growing old; you've just reached that vibrant metallic age: silver in your hair, gold in your teeth, and lead in your bottom![241]

BARBARA JOHNSON

WEEKEND

❖

TRAVELING CHUMS

As iron sharpens iron,
  so one man sharpens another.

G iven first dibs on travel companions, I would pick
Thelma, Luci, Marilyn, Sheila, and Barbara right off
the bat. Thelma often is tucked in a corner behind the scenes,
Bible spread open, preparing herself for ministry. Luci can
guide us into stimulating conversations as well with her witty,
thought-provoking questions.

Marilyn keeps us all chortling and challenged with her
comedic sense and her insightful offerings. Sheila's brilliant
mind, lightning-quick humor, and sterling devotion brighten
my path. Barbara's a seasoned journeyer who has taught me
how to travel on with smiles in my miles.

Who are your traveling chums? Do they promote smiles
in your miles? Do they add joy to your journey? When we
choose companions, may we be wise and select those who are
wholesome, humorous, helpful, and honorable.[242]

PATSY CLAIRMONT

Heavenly Father, thank you for the wonderful friends
you've given me, each with her own unique perspective,
personality, and gifts. Use us to sharpen one another, to
encourage each other in our spiritual growth. Amen.

244   PROMISES OF JOY

MONDAY

A GENTLE HEART

Thou hast also given me the shield of thy salvation:
and thy right hand hath holden me up,
and thy gentleness hath made me great.

PSALM 18:35 KJV

Forgiving ourselves is hard. But until we do, I don't believe we can fully forgive anyone else. It's accepting that we're not enough—and never will be—and being okay with that. Then we can accept others, knowing they are not enough, either, and we can still have a gentle heart.

In the New Testament, the most common Greek word for *gentle* is *prautes*. In *The Complete Word Study Dictionary: New Testament,* Spiros Zodhiates translates it as "an inward grace of the soul, a calmness toward God in particular. It is the acceptance of God's dealings with us, considering them as good in that they enhance the closeness of our relationship with him."

In *Living Beyond Yourself,* Beth Moore describes gentleness as complete surrender to God's will and way in our life. "To stop fighting God. It is quite the opposite of weakness. Meekness and gentleness is the power and strength created from submitting to God's will."[243]

A gentle heart is a joyful heart.

SHEILA WALSH

TUESDAY

THE BLESSED GOD

*God, the blessed and only Ruler, the King of kings
and Lord of lords, who alone is immortal and
who lives in unapproachable light.*

1 TIMOTHY 6:15–16

To be blessed is to be happy. Actually, the scholars use the word *blissful* for blessed. Exultant and joyous, radiant and rapturous. God is not a threatened, pacing deity starving for attention. He is not easily angered, touchy, or out of sorts on bad days. He is not biting his nails or blowing his stack when the world goes awry. Rather, he is the exultant and rapturously happy God.

That's good news. If we're in trouble, God had better not be. If we're miserable, it would do us no good to go to Someone who's also miserable. People in deep distress need to reach out and find a strong, secure, and happy anchor. God is just that: a joyful foundation, a blissful rock, a happy fortress. We never need to worry about whether he got up on the wrong side of the bed only to face us with an angry growl. Nothing we do can disturb the blessedness of God—we will always find him full of compassion and tender mercies.[244]

JONI EARECKSON TADA

WEDNESDAY

❁

THE STONE WITH
A BROKEN HEART

The LORD is close to the brokenhearted
and saves those who are crushed in spirit.

PSALM 34:18

The opal is a stone with a broken heart. Made of dust, sand, and silica, it is full of minute fissures that allow air to be trapped inside. The trapped air refracts the light, resulting in the lovely hues that inspire the opal's nickname, the Lamp of Fire. When kept in a cold, dark place, the opal loses its luster. But when held in a warm hand or when the light shines on it, the luster is restored. So it is with us. A broken heart becomes a lamp of fire when we allow God to breathe on it and warm us with his life.

If things are tough, remember that every flower that ever bloomed had to go through a whole lot of dirt to get there. Our Father will use life's reversals to move you forward toward joy. Regret will not prevent tomorrow's sorrows; it will only rob today of its strength. So keep on believing. With Jesus, you have not a hopeless end but an endless hope![245]

BARBARA JOHNSON

THURSDAY

ALTOGETHER LOVELY

His mouth is sweetness itself;
  he is altogether lovely.
This is my lover, this my friend.

SONG OF SONGS 5:16

Even if you're not really in love right now, you can probably recall what it felt like. Your heart grows faint and your breathing short just picturing the soft eyes and tender smile of the one you adore. Being in the same room is a thrill. When you're in love, one thing is for certain: You can't keep it to yourself. You just have to tell that person who grips your affection.

Likewise, we are happier and more complete when we express our love for God in praise. Express your love for God in a way you seldom choose: sing a (solo!) praise song to him, write him a love letter, put some balloons on your porch as a symbol of your love. Grab a hymnal and go outside when the moon is full this month—flip to the hymn "Jesus, Lover of My Soul" and happily praise him. Let your heart direct you to an idea that delights you. It will delight God, too.[246]

JONI EARECKSON TADA

FRIDAY

MAKE SOMEONE'S DAY

The right word at the right time
is like golden apples in silver jewelry.

PROVERBS 25:11 NIRV

Picture this: You are asked to travel for most of the week-ends of an entire year around the country with five women you've never met. You'll be speaking, eating, and praying together. You'll be under pressure together, and you'll share in the joys and tribulations of traveling together. That's an awful lot of togetherness with a bunch of strangers, if you ask me.

If I had known what it was going to be like to travel with these five Women of Faith, I would have signed up sooner. I had no idea how exciting and vibrant they were, nor what an influence they would have on my life. Through all the pain, sorrow, disappointment, aggravation, and agitation of life, these wonderful women are still funny, adventurous, and silly.

You, too, can be a blessing to the people you meet today. Life has its serious moments. But being a bit kooky may be the secret to seeing yourself and others through good times and bad. Go ahead, make someone's day.[247]

THELMA WELLS

WEEKEND

JOY OVERFLOWING

Jesus said, "Blessed are the poor in spirit,
for theirs is the kingdom of heaven....
Blessed are the meek,
for they will inherit the earth....
Blessed are the peacemakers,
for they will be called sons of God."

MATTHEW 5:3, 5, 9

Jesus had joy and happiness in mind when he said, "Blessed are the poor...the meek...the peacemakers." He meant that such people are divinely favored; they are smiled upon; they are truly the delightfully contented ones. We are most like God when we are full of joy—godly joy that overflows from meekness, humility, and spiritual poverty—that is, a deep awareness of our desperate need of him.

Are you overflowing with the joy of God? Ask him to fill you until you are full to the top and can't contain another drop.[248]

JONI EARECKSON TADA

Heavenly Father, may I feel the overflow of your joy today.
May I see myself as blessed, happy, and delightfully
contented in you. I come to you acknowledging my need
and ready to receive all the joy you wish to pour out
on me. Remind me to pass the overflow on to others. Amen.

MONDAY

WELCOME HOME

*Everyone who calls on the name of the Lord
will be saved.*

ROMANS 10:13

I was once a guest singer at a Billy Graham crusade. Billy's message was simple and uncompromising. No bells or whistles "wowed" the crowd, just a simple call was made to "come home." I wondered what the response would be. I wondered if the message sounded too good to be true. I wondered if it sounded too simple.

But then it began——people streaming to the front to receive Christ. I had to bury my face in my hands, overwhelmed with pure joy at being a spectator to such a homecoming.

It would be such a shame to sit in church every Sunday and listen to what's being said about God but never grasp that this is a personal invitation——a welcome mat just for you. All you have to do is pray: Thank God for loving you. Thank him for sending Jesus to die on the cross for you. Tell him you want to "come home." He'll be waiting for you.[249]

SHEILA WALSH

TUESDAY

GETTING AWAY FROM IT ALL

The LORD makes me lie down in green pastures,
*   he leads me beside quiet waters,*
*   he restores my soul.*

PSALM 23:2–3

Mmmm…So good to get away from the everyday of life. Perfect solitude. Time to reflect, read, write, and pray.

God has manifested himself in breathtaking sunsets and a dancing porpoise show. "Together now, up and out of the water. Smile and dive," say the porpoise. "Under the boat and out. Higher this time. They love us!"

Today we saw a rainbow—a complete rainbow. We considered sailing off to find the pot of gold. But whatever would we do with a pot of gold? And who would believe our story?

Tonight we made up silly songs and poetry, even a joint venturing one about the captain of our ship. We were silly beyond words.

And to think we almost didn't come. "Too busy," we said. Busy doing what? It slips my mind just now.[250] Sheer joy.

SUE BUCHANAN

WEDNESDAY

❋

THE GUTSIEST DECISION
YOU CAN MAKE

Bear with each other and forgive whatever
grievances you may have against one another.
Forgive as the Lord forgave you.

COLOSSIANS 3:13

Have you heard of International Forgiveness Week? Sure enough, I found it on the calendar, smack-dab in the middle of winter. In winter you feel dull, drab, and closed in, as though spring will never come. You are restless, cold, and irritable—the way you feel when you hold a grudge.

Forgiveness enables you to bury your grudge in the icy earth and put the past behind you. You flush resentment away by being the first to forgive. Forgiveness fashions your future. The gutsiest decision you can make. As you forgive others, winter will soon make way for springtime as fresh joy pushes up through the soil of your heart.

Forgiveness is a stunning principle, your ticket out of hate and fear and chaos. I know what regret feels like. But I also know what forgiveness feels like, because God has so graciously forgiven me. Forgiveness frees you of the past so you can make good choices today. Look to Jesus as your example.[251]

BARBARA JOHNSON

THURSDAY

THE LORD IS GOOD

Give thanks to the LORD, for he is good;
    his love endures forever.
Let the redeemed of the LORD say this.

PSALM 107:1—2

It was a dull Saturday. My spirits were drooping, and it was all I could do to fight off depression. A corset riding high was digging into my ribs, forcing me to draw deep breaths now and then. And when I did, I would say, "The Lord is good." Somewhere after the fifth "Lord is good," my friend turned and gave a good-natured dig, asking, "What are you doing? Trying to convince yourself?"

"You've got it," I replied. It's not that I doubted God's goodness; I simply wanted to remind my dry, cracked soul of the truth. It's easy to announce God's goodness when your spirits are soaring; it's another thing—a more God-glorifying thing—to proclaim the goodness of God out loud when you're under the weather.

Voicing the goodness of God is a testimony not only to your downcast soul but to others listening in. Find moments today to speak joyfully of the goodness of God, no matter what your emotions insist.[252]

JONI EARECKSON TADA

FRIDAY

TREASURES OF THE KINGDOM OF GOD

The kingdom of God is not a matter of eating and drinking, but of righteousness, peace and joy in the Holy Spirit.

ROMANS 14:17

It's time to get to grace, to joy, to peace. It's what we are longing for and what we have been promised. This is to be the hallmark of our lives as God's children. It's not something we can work up by ourselves. It has to grow.

The amazing thing is that it grows in such an unfriendly climate. You stick a mother in an intensive care unit watching over her child—and the last thing you'd expect is peace. But there it is all over her, mixed in with the tears and the sadness. You take a man's job away from him, the source of a significant portion of his identity, his ability to take care of his family—and peace would seem out of place, even unwelcome. But there it is. I have seen it so many times.[253]

Avail yourself of these treasures of the kingdom of God. Not only will they enhance your life, but they will shine as beacons to a lost and dying world.

SHEILA WALSH

WEEKEND

✣

SHEER JOY

Jesus said, "What I'm about to tell you is true.
You need to change and become like little children.
If you don't, you will never enter the kingdom of heaven."

MATTHEW 18:3 NIRV

W hen was the last time you did something childlike out of sheer joy? Said something childlike? If today's thoughts energize you, express your delight in God in the way a child would: fingerpaint a wild and colorful poster, sing at the top of your lungs a song you learned in Sunday school, buy a Tootsie-Pop and lick it for fun. Most of all do a little kingdom play, telling God in song, word, or deed how delighted you are in him.

God loves you, and he wants you to enjoy being in his presence. Rest in that, and have a little fun![254]

JONI EARECKSON TADA

Heavenly Father, being in your presence is a delight
like no other on earth. I feel light and giggly and full
of joy. Receive my song as I bring it to you now.
It comes from my heart. Thank you for the privilege
of relaxing and enjoying our time together. Amen.

Monday

Celebrate All Your Days

All the days of the oppressed are wretched,
but the cheerful heart has a continual feast.

PROVERBS 15:15

I like having special days, days set aside to commemorate happy events: birthdays, anniversaries, graduations. My journals are full of remembrances like, "Forty years ago today my parents were married." Or, "Remember, Luci, three years ago you bought this house."

Days are important. I anticipate them. I'm looking forward to the day my friends come for Thanksgiving, to the next time I'll see my brother in Florida.

The word *days* appears more than five hundred times in Scripture, and the Mosaic Law prescribed feast days when the congregation was to celebrate by dancing, singing, resting from labor, and giving praise to God. These were occasions of joy and gladness.

I encourage you to create special days for yourself and your family. Twenty-four hours when you do something entirely different from other days...or maybe do nothing at all.

This is the day the Lord has made. Rejoice. Celebrate all your days.[255]

LUCI SWINDOLL

TUESDAY

CULTIVATE YOUR
GARDEN OF LOVE

Those who sow righteousness get a true reward.

PROVERBS 11:18 NRSV

It seems as though everyone is a gardener, even if they live in a big-city apartment. Even if they wouldn't pull weeds for a million dollars. Even if they don't know the difference between a spade and a rake. Even if they hate vegetables and bugs, are allergic to bees, or have spring allergies. Suddenly everyone is a gardening maniac.

Well, there are certain things anybody can plant—sweet Ps in a straight row, for instance: prayer, patience, peace, passion. But it's not enough for a gardener to love flowers. A gardener also must hate weeds. As good plants grow, you pinch off bitter ones like panic, paranoia, and passivity. And by the way, while gardening, do squash pride. And please, lettuce love one another at all times.

Begin now to cultivate your half-acre of love. All it takes is a few seeds no larger than grains of sand. The blossom of a good deed fades with time, but that lasting perfume is the joy you receive from doing it.[256]

BARBARA JOHNSON

WEDNESDAY

✺

KINGDOM PLAY

Jesus said, "Let the little children come to me...
for the kingdom of heaven belongs to such as these."

MATTHEW 19:14

I'll never forget the first time someone showed me in the Bible that I would one day have a new, glorified body. "You're kidding!" I said in wonder. We cross-referenced other passages, and sure enough, it was there as plain as day. "You mean, I'll be able to walk and run? Not be a spacey spirit-being with no legs or arms?" My joy was so great that my friend pushed me outside in my wheelchair (it was near midnight), and we hooted and howled at the full moon. He circled my chair around and around, and we "danced" with glee over the kingdom promises we'd just read.

I call it kingdom play. It happens when you experience an "Aha!" moment of delight in God. It bursts beyond happiness and calls for rejoicing out of sheer generosity. Like a child, you just *have* to go outside, beyond the four walls of normal human experience, and play![257]

JONI EARECKSON TADA

THURSDAY

❋

DON'T GIVE UP ON THEM

*The prayer of a godly person is powerful. It makes
things happen.*

JAMES 5:16 NIRV

O ne of the most colorful people in my family is Uncle
Lawrence Morris, Jr. His nickname is Uncle Brother.
Although he had accepted Christ as a young man, Uncle
Brother had lived like the devil. But I prayed for him to
return to the Lord. I didn't want him to die without realizing
he could enjoy a better life than the one he had chosen.

Thanks be to God, for the past several years, Uncle Brother
has made some major changes. He reads his Bible, bridles his
tongue, has changed his friends. He is concerned about others.

God was always present, waiting for him to reopen his heart.

Are you dealing with someone whom you feel will never
change? Nobody is so far from God that he can't get back to
the Lord. Our responsibility is to keep believing God will
answer our prayers. Thank God for what he will do. Patiently
but expectantly wait on the Lord.[258] Think of the joy you and
that person will share throughout eternity.

THELMA WELLS

Friday

ACCEPTED IN THE BELOVED

To the praise of the glory of his grace,
wherein he hath made us accepted in the beloved.

EPHESIANS 1:6 KJV

I used to find it hard to make deep friendships. I felt such a need for approval and acceptance; yet I was afraid to let the real me be seen in case I wasn't good enough. The higher I erected a façade, the more I needed approval, but the less I was available to receive it. Hiding behind that wall, I didn't realize how much effort it would take for someone to scale those heights to find the real, scared, and unsure me.

Finally, I figured out I was inadequate to create or maintain relationships. Fortunately, I realized Christ is enough for all of us. His mercy helps us to see others mercifully, and his loving acceptance of us enables us to accept ourselves and others. With that as a beginning point, we can relax, be ourselves, and come out from behind the protective walls we've erected. Then we can connect with others who have discovered the joy of just being themselves—flawed and silly but of worth because of Jesus.[259]

SHEILA WALSH

WEEKEND

BETTER AND BETTER

*The path of the righteous is like the first gleam of dawn,
shining ever brighter till the full light of day.*

PROVERBS 4:18

My father, forever in faded jeans, red suspenders, and plaid shirt, looked so uncomfortable when he'd come to the hospital to see me back in those early days of my injury. It warmed my heart when he'd whisper with wet eyes, "In every day and in every way, you're getting better and better and better."

My body never shook off the paralysis. The pragmatist would say, "See, your father's words were wishful thinking. You didn't get better, Joni; instead you got stuck with a wheelchair." But I believe my daddy was right. Every day I did get better. Maybe not on the outside, but on the inside. My soul became settled; my joy returned.

Think of the last time you said, "Lord, it would be better if…" It's not that God has a different definition for the word *better;* it's just that his idea of better goes deeper. It goes to the heart of the matter.[260]

JONI EARECKSON TADA

*Heavenly Father, because you are a good God, I can trust you.
Cause me to grow better and better in you every day. Amen.*

MONDAY

LET YOUR JOY OUT

My lips will shout for joy
when I sing praise to you—
I, whom you have redeemed.
My tongue will tell of your righteous acts
all day long.

PSALM 71:23–24

I've decided to get into a good humor and stay that way. I want to treat people with kindness and a smile, regardless of how they treat me. The smile, the kindness, comes back.

Let your joy out. One way I do that is to give people something to laugh about. I collect jokes and write down everything that makes me brighten up. I make amusement a ministry because chuckles are better than a therapist. They are aloe vera for the sunburns of life. When the dumps take their toll, laughter provides the exact change to get you through.

Whatever your troubles, try looking at them by the light of a different star. Find a wacky angle, a new twist. Offer trouble a little serious thought, then turn it upside down and look at it through God-colored glasses. Chew on trouble's possibilities for making you smarter, better, stronger, kinder. Then take the curved weapon I call joy, and toss trouble by its funny side out into the world.[261]

BARBARA JOHNSON

TUESDAY

DID YOU KNOW?

Dear friends, do not be surprised at the painful trial you are suffering, as though something strange were happening to you.

1 PETER 4:12

Did you know what you were getting into when you became a believer? The question isn't all that important now that you've signed up. What's important is that you not be surprised at the fiery trial—it comes so that through it, you might take up your cross and follow Jesus. It comes so that you might find your life after you lose it.

When I first came to Christ, I sort of knew it meant suffering, but I had no idea it would involve paralysis. I was surprised at the painful trial at first, thinking something strange had happened to me. But now I praise God for this wheelchair. It has taken me down Calvary's path. It's the path to deep-down joy and peace.[262]

Maybe it's time for you to take another look at your trials—see them from God's perspective, and rejoice in what God is able to do through them.

JONI EARECKSON TADA

WEDNESDAY

❋

LETTING GO

I desire to do your will, O my God;
  your law is within my heart.

There's the saying in Alcoholics Anonymous that there is *your* will and *God's* will—and your will doesn't matter! My friend Steve Lorenz and I talk about the outrageous freedom this reality brings. Can you imagine the peace that would result from this kind of letting go? No matter what comes into our day, we relinquish our desire to strike back, to vindicate, to look good, to shame another, to let anger take hold, to have our own way. I get so bogged down in the frustrating specifics of life that I lose sight of the goal: *to become more like Christ.* As long as I see myself as a slave to the whims and moods of others, I will sink in the slough of despond. But when I let go and trust that God is in control, I can fly—even with broken wings. How happy it must make God when one of his children lives and loves with this level of understanding and grace.[263]

SHEILA WALSH

THURSDAY

❋

DIVINE JOY

God saw that it was good.

GENESIS 1:18

Isn't it great to step back from a project well completed and just enjoy the joy? You've seen the happiness in a child's face whose crayon masterpiece gets taped to the fridge. It's the same contentment and joy you feel after serving the applauded turkey dinner or admiring the row of pansies you planted along the wall.

Now imagine the pleasure God derives from everything he has made. What do you think surged through him the minute after a billion galaxies burst into being? After standing back to take in the panorama, God rested—not to catch his breath from exhaustion but to savor the moment and revel in the pleasure of what he created.

Think of what surges through God's heart when you—his epitome of creation—make it your ambition to be pleasing to him, aspiring to fulfill all his greatest desires for you. Be assured that when you please him, you *really* please him, with a joy that is humanly indescribable.[264]

JONI EARECKSON TADA

FRIDAY

A LAUGH LIFESTYLE

May the Lord of peace himself give you peace at all times and in every way. The Lord be with all of you.

2 THESSALONIANS 3:16

I'm often asked to give pointers on how to develop a laugh lifestyle. I always find that a difficult question because a laugh lifestyle is so much more than joke books, funny tapes, or humorous movies. They have their place and can certainly provide wonderful times of laughter, but the humor they inspire comes from the outside.

The development of a laugh lifestyle begins internally with a foundation that is God-inspired and God-constructed. Faith is that solid foundation that leads to personal rest and divine security. Without this internal peace, the laughter inspired by all the zany antics we can think of will ultimately die in the wind, leaving a hollow void waiting to be filled with the next antic or joke.

I guess it all comes down to this: The key to developing a laugh lifestyle is to become personally acquainted with the Author and Giver of joy. His name is Jesus.[265]

MARILYN MEBERG

WEEKEND

No Scars in Heaven?

Jesus said to Thomas, "Put your finger here;
see my hands. Reach out your hand and put it
into my side. Stop doubting and believe."

JOHN 20:27

Will Jesus bear his scars in heaven? Revelation 5:6 describes the scene: "I saw a Lamb, *looking as if it had been slain*, standing in the center of the throne." I have an inkling he will be the *only* one who will retain the painful reminders of his earthly journey. We, on the other hand, will bear no scars. All our tears will be wiped away. The scars of Jesus will not be painful for us to see but will be an eternal reason to rejoice.

Why wait for heaven to rejoice? Today the Lord accommodates himself to help you through doubts. He'll go to great lengths to help confirm your faith. He invites you to place your hand in his and feel what it cost to purchase your salvation.[266]

JONI EARECKSON TADA

Lord Jesus, help me to have faith through the crisis
I'm in right now. Remind me of all the evidence
you have provided that I might believe. Amen.

MONDAY

❋

RESCUED FROM REGRET

*If we confess our sins, he is faithful and just and will
forgive us our sins and purify us from all unrighteousness.*

1 JOHN 1:9

A saboteur of joy is the many ways we are disappointed
with ourselves. We live with regrets that drag us down,
sometimes to the depths of despair.

Many of us who have been Christians for years get up
every morning intending to serve and please God, and yet,
with the apostle Paul, we do what we don't want to do. We
miss the mark and then live in regret.

I think of the apostle Paul—a Christian—admitting his
own weakness: "What a wretched man I am! Who will rescue
me from this body of death?" That question is followed by an
exclamation: "Thanks be to God—through Jesus Christ our
Lord!" (Romans 7:24–25). Jesus is the only One who can rescue me from myself.

God knows about the secret abortion, the private fantasy
life, the hatred you hold in your heart. It is only when we confess these things to God that he can fill the broken, empty
places with his joy.[267]

SHEILA WALSH

TUESDAY

IT'S BETTER TOGETHER

Praise the Lord from the earth ...
  young men and maidens,
  old men and children.

PSALM 148:7, 12

Would you look at this? Isn't it wonderful?!" My coworker Angela always beckons me away from my desk at the end of the day whenever a beautiful sunset emblazons the coastal hills by our office. She simply must share her joy with others. And that's what praise is all about, isn't it? When we consider some aspect of life praiseworthy, whether it's a sunset, a baby's smile, or a beautiful new painting we just hung in the living room, our delight is multiplied when others enjoy that special something with us.

Find some aspect of nature—the texture of the tree trunk in the backyard, or a blue jay's brilliant feathers—and then rejoice in it with someone else. Consider together some glorious aspect of God. Maybe his mighty work in creation will come to mind. Or his attention to details. Or his infinite array of colors in creation. The point is to praise him with someone else. [268]

JONI EARECKSON TADA

WEDNESDAY

❋

BEYOND-THE-CALL-OF-DUTY FRIENDSHIP

*Carry each other's burdens, and in this way
you will fulfill the law of Christ.*

GALATIANS 6:2

R ecently I moved—only seven blocks, but I still had to
pick up everything and find a place to set it down in my
new abode—that or have an enormous (thirty-four years'
worth of stuff) yard sale. Thankfully, I had dear friends come
to my rescue and help me pack.

After arriving in our new home, I was overwhelmed. I
had thought I would pull it together rapidly. Instead, I
roamed from room to room trying to remember my name.
Carol came to give support (and to verify my identity) for
four days. She assisted me until early evening, when she
would then make our dinner, serve us, and clean up. You can
only guess what a gift that was to me. I never expected that
kind of beyond-the-call-of-duty effort, but I'm certain our
new home would have found me sinking before I could even
unload the cargo, if it were not for Carol's life preserver of
kindness.[269] Much-needed help from a good friend warms
the heart with joy.

PATSY CLAIRMONT

THURSDAY

❋

THE EASTER SPIRIT

*Grieve, mourn and wail. Change your
laughter to mourning and your joy to gloom.
Humble yourselves before the Lord, and he will lift you up.*

JAMES 4:9–10

Y ou hardly ever hear people talking about getting into the spirit of Easter. And there's a good reason why. If the Easter season is to have a spirit about it, it's the spirit of repentance. Only when we contemplate the full weight of our transgressions can we genuinely celebrate all that happened on Resurrection Sunday. When we consider the depth of our depravity, we are able to fully enjoy the height of our happiness over Christ's victory from the grave. Our joy is only as real, deep, and sincere as our grief over our sin—otherwise we have no idea what he's saved us from.

The Easter spirit can't be mustered up with baskets of eggs, chocolate rabbits, hot cross buns, or honey-baked hams. This stuff has about as much connection to the real meaning of Lent as Santa Claus has to Christmas. To get into the spirit of this season, ask yourself, *What thing, habit, person, or fantasy—what is it I can bring to the cross?*[270]

JONI EARECKSON TADA

FRIDAY

CHANGE THE BRICK WALL TO GOD

*Jesus said, "Come to me, all you who are weary
and burdened, and I will give you rest. Take my yoke
upon you and learn from me, for I am gentle and
humble in heart, and you will find rest for your souls."*

MATTHEW 11:28–29

Whenever I find myself feeling weary and overwhelmed by the commitments I've made, I remember Jesus' words: "From everyone who has been given much, much will be demanded; and from the one who has been entrusted with much, much more will be asked" (Luke 12:48). I know God didn't bless me so I could sit back and keep them all to myself.

Sometimes life becomes so complicated we feel as if we've gone as far as we can down this stressful highway. We imagine ourselves smashed up against a brick wall, unable to answer one more call, hear one more complaint, or even take one more breath. When that's the image that fills your mind, change the brick wall to God. Imagine yourself pressed tightly against his heart, wrapped in his everlasting arms, soothed by his life-giving breath. Picture yourself encircled in God's love, soaked in his strength. Then step out onto the highway once more.[271] You'll be refreshed, and your joy will return.

BARBARA JOHNSON

WEEKEND

❋

COUNT IT ALL JOY

Jesus said, "Blessed are you when people insult you, persecute you and falsely say all kinds of evil against you because of me. Rejoice and be glad, because great is your reward in heaven, for in the same way they persecuted the prophets who were before you."

PSALM 89:16–17

Have you ever been asked to suffer for your faith in God? If not, you are truly fortunate. Throughout our modern world, Christians are being persecuted—some even losing their lives—each and every day.

Thomas Watson offered these encouraging words more than 300 years ago:

Persons who wade through deep water fix their eyes upon the firm land before them. They that bear the cross patiently shall wear the crown triumphantly. Not all the silks of Persia, the spices of Arabia, and the gold of Ophir can be compared to this glorious reward! This glorious reward in heaven is called a reigning with Christ (2 Timothy 2:12). The wicked first reign, and then suffer. The godly first suffer, and then reign.

THOMAS WATSON

Heavenly Father, I rejoice in my relationship with you. Any suffering I might encounter as a result, I will count as joy. I will keep my eyes fixed on the glorious reward you have prepared for me at the end of my journey. Amen.

MONDAY

LIVE TO CHRIST,
LIVE FOR ONE ANOTHER

Be completely humble and gentle; be patient,
bearing with one another in love. Make every effort to
keep the unity of the Spirit through the bond of peace.

EPHESIANS 4:2–3

My father-in-law has recently lost his wife, yet he describes his life at the moment as "the best days of my life." What is it that would evoke such a wonderful proclamation?

Part of it is obvious. He lives with his only son, whom he loves dearly, and his only grandson, whom he indulges copiously! He and I are good friends, too. But there is more at work here. We are learning together how to live in community as those who treasure one another. We get it wrong a lot, but we always say "sorry." We are learning that the corporate good is bigger than what each individual wants.

We are not a house of martyrs, but we are learning to relinquish our so-called rights in order to love each other well. When we all fly in formation, life is joy. When we live like this, we can *all* say, "These are the best days of our lives."272

SHEILA WALSH

TUESDAY

A LIST OF TEARS

Record my lament;
list my tears on your scroll—
are they not in your record?

PSALM 56:8

Think of all the tears you've ever cried. That time at recess when you weren't picked for dodge ball. That Saturday night of the prom when you sat home alone. The job interview that went sour. The time your neighbor down the street told you to "quit talking about religion." The day your father died. The day your spouse left.

You may have thought no one noticed your red eyes. Not so. God saw. What's more, he has every intention of rewarding your endurance through that pain. Why else would he meticulously chronicle every one of your tears?

Every tear you've cried—think of it—will be redeemed. God will give you indescribable joy for your grief. Not with a general wave of the hand—but rather, each tear has been listed; each will be recompensed.

Make a list of the times you've cried from hurt, disappointment, or physical pain in the last few years, and thank God for redeeming each tear with a season of joy.[273]

JONI EARECKSON TADA

WEDNESDAY

✸

DON'T SWEAT
THE BIG STUFF, EITHER

*Jesus said, "I have told you these things, so that in me
you may have peace. In this world you will have
trouble. But take heart! I have overcome the world."*

JOHN 16:33

Let's face it: Some things in life are BIG. SERIOUS.
SCARY. Maybe you're going through a painful
divorce...or looking forward to getting married. Perhaps
you're expecting a child...or wrestling for the soul of one
you've already got. Maybe you're struggling with your health
or finances, and every corner you turn seems to thrust you
into a new battle zone.

So what's a woman to do? Pretend it's not as bad as it is?
Moan and groan? Gird your loins and ride into battle? Hightail
it and run? God has a better way. A way that allows us to hold
on to our joy no matter what heartbreaks or anxieties or
opportunities we face. It's a way that has nothing to do with us
and everything to do with him.

If you're facing some big stuff, you need not let your fear
dictate your feelings and actions. Your big stuff may indeed be
big...but God is bigger.[274]

TRACI MULLINS

THURSDAY

❖

THE BEAUTY OF THE EARTH

Can you bind the beautiful Pleiades?
  Can you loose the cords of Orion?
Can you bring forth the constellations in their seasons
  or lead out the Bear with its cubs?

JOB 38:31-32

I showed up early at church one evening and found the front door locked. As I sat outside and enjoyed the stars, Chris, a college student, drove up.

As we waited together, I pointed out to Chris the various constellations. "Chris," I said, "did you know Orion is mentioned in the Bible?"

Later I showed him Job 38:31. To put it mildly, he was pleasantly surprised. All the beauty of the earth, the glories of the night sky, the fields, the birds, all this magnificent beauty is God's. It's not the property of astrologers, naturalists, Greenpeace, or new agers. It's all owned by the Lord. And it's another reason to praise him.

Go outside and look around you. Find five things in nature for which to praise God. And if that's too easy, look for ten. He has surrounded us with bounteous beauty—and a myriad of reasons to joyfully sing his praises.[275]

JONI EARECKSON TADA

FRIDAY

THE BLESSING OF FELLOWSHIP

*Let us not give up meeting together, as some are in
the habit of doing, but let us encourage one another—
and all the more as you see the Day approaching.*

HEBREWS 10:25

I'm convinced that Christian fellowship is mandatory for
my heart and soul. Nothing can take its place.

One day outside a church in Buenos Aires, the spirited
sounds of singing and clapping met us on the sidewalk,
enveloped us, and literally propelled us forward. We were surrounded by radiantly smiling Latin faces singing praises to God
with utter abandon. Not only was I moved by the powerful
presence of the Holy Spirit in that place, but I also realized how
rejuvenated I felt to be enveloped by believers. It felt wonderful to be bathed in the oneness of these dear Christians, who
hugged and kissed us with such unaffected genuineness. That
sweet Sunday will live forever in my memory, as I reflect on fellowship that was unhindered by language or cultural barriers.

Spend time with fellow believers rejoicing over what you
have in Jesus. Sing some songs. Laugh together. Pray for one
another. Hug each other. Celebrate the blessed tie that binds you
to one another in Christian love.[276]

MARILYN MEBERG

WEEKEND

PICTURE IT!

Even though you have not seen him, you love him.
Though you do not see him now, you believe in him.
You are filled with a glorious joy that can't be put
into words.

1 PETER 1:8 NIRV

I realize you and I have never seen Jesus, but nothing's preventing us from picturing him. Try this exercise. Right now, where you are sitting, think about where the door is. Behind you? To the side of where you sit? Now as you continue reading, imagine the Lord Jesus coming up the hallway or the path outside your door. Now, see in your mind's eye the Lord moving into your room. He's in no hurry. Perhaps he folds his arms, smiles, and observes you for a moment. He comes closer and sits down beside you.

You love the Lord Jesus and trust him, even though you have never seen him. Do today's exercise occasionally to train your thinking that, yes, the Lord Jesus is near and ever-present, even though he is invisible to your eyes. You'll be blessed with a joy that comes from heaven itself.[277]

JONI EARECKSON TADA

Heavenly Father, I don't have to see you to love you
or know that you are real. Your Word is enough
until I meet you face-to-face. Amen.

MONDAY

THE LEADING OF THE HOLY SPIRIT

Those who are led by the Spirit of God are the children of God.

ROMANS 8:14 TNIV

My experience with the prompting of the Holy Spirit has been that when he directs you, there is an indescribable peace in your body, mind, and spirit that you feel but can't explain to anyone who hasn't experienced it. God's Spirit would never direct us to do anything contrary to Scripture, so we have a guidebook that can help us, too.

You've probably said, "I knew in my heart that such and such was …" Those are probably times God's Spirit was prompting you.

I need to be responsive to the Holy Spirit. I have found him to be the greatest organizer, time manager, administrator, and scheduler.

What will you do when you think you're being prompted by the Holy Spirit to take a certain action? I'd suggest you ask for clarity. Wait for the answer. I can't tell you how you will know when the answer comes, but I can tell you that you will experience peace. Listen to your heart.[278] There is joy in following the Holy Spirit.

THELMA WELLS

TUESDAY

IT'S THAT SIMPLE

Godliness with contentment is great gain.

1 TIMOTHY 6:6

I want to ask you some questions," the pastor said to Jani, holding her in his arms. "Do you love your mom and dad, and do they love you?"

"Uh-huh," Jani said with a nod, smiling shyly.

"And do you love Jesus, and does he love you?"

"Uh-huh."

The pastor turned to the congregation. "A little jealous, aren't you?" Jani climbed down and ran back to her dad's lap, giggling.

Jealous of what? We're jealous of Jani's contentment. Her "uh-huh" speaks volumes. The complexities of life have vanished, and she lives a life of simple joy and contentment.

"But Jani's just a child," you say. "My life isn't—and can't be—that simple." Don't believe it. Your heavenly Father—infinitely more capable than Jani's parents—considers her childlike contentment to be of infinite value. You will have gained infinite joy when you live a godly life and answer the world's fundamental question, *Are you happy?* with a direct smile and affirmation like Jani's. Try saying it…"Uh-huh."[279]

JONI EARECKSON TADA

WEDNESDAY

❋

EASTER PEOPLE

Among the people of the world you shine like stars in the heavens. You shine as you hold out to them the word of life.

PHILIPPIANS 2:15–16 NIRV

I believe the world is shaped by the hand of a loving God. The Bible shows that we are an Easter people living in a Good Friday world, not Good Friday people living in an Easter world. That means we are destined for joy, no matter how difficult our daily life. Something in us responds to the happiness other people experience, because we glimpse life as God intends it to be! It is an image imprinted in the spirit of Easter morning—pure, powerful, and potent, like the resurrection.

So go out there and help create all the happy endings you can. Don't be afraid of tears. You will have your share of Good Fridays, but Easter will come. Remember, moist eyes are good. Trembling lips are acceptable. Quivering voices won't hurt anybody. Tears are signals there is something deeper to be understood.

Go ahead and let the tears flow. But know, too, that the blue of heaven is far bigger than any gray clouds beneath.[280]

BARBARA JOHNSON

WEEKEND

❋

A SACRIFICE OF PRAISE

Through Jesus, therefore, let us continually offer to God a sacrifice of praise—the fruit of lips that confess his name. And do not forget to do good and to share with others, for with such sacrifices God is pleased.

HEBREWS 13:15–16

Ken and I worship in a small church. The Pomeroy family, including the youngest, Veronica, usually sits a few rows in front of us. Veronica likes to wear pretty hats over her blond hair. She also coughs a lot. I used to think she was plagued by frequent colds. I later learned she has cystic fibrosis, a severe lung disease that clogs her breathing passages with phlegm.

I sometimes watch Veronica during worship service. Especially when we sing hymns. She gasps in between the lines, and I wonder what God must be thinking as he receives her praise. Actually, I already know: "With such sacrifices God is pleased." More than pleased. God's greatness is magnified when Veronica determines to wheeze her way through a hymn—her gutsy praise demonstrates how *special* she thinks God is.

God is pleased with the praise you give him, but he swells with joy when the praise he breathes has the aroma of your sweet-smelling sacrifice.[281]

JONI EARECKSON TADA

Monday

The Prodigal Son in Reverse

Jesus said, "The father said to his servants,
"Let's have a feast and celebrate. For this son of mine
was dead and is alive again; he was lost and is found."'

Luke 15:22–24

What Jesus Christ has done for us is something the best writers, producers, and directors could never come up with. He left all he had in order to come and embrace us in our filthy rags. He cleans us up—but he doesn't leave us there. He takes us home to live with him forever. It's like the story of the Prodigal Son in reverse. Christ, the Son who had it all, came to us in a far country and gave up his inheritance for us. Now he stands at his Father's right hand as the elder brother, but as the one who *welcomes* us home—even though we were the ones who frittered away his inheritance. And with his Father, he watches for us, and when he sees us on the horizon, he runs to welcome us home.

Referring to Christ's return to heaven, Frere Pierre Marie says, from the perspective of the Father, "My Prodigal Son is home, and he has brought them all back with him!"[282]

Sheila Walsh

WEEKEND

A PRESCRIPTION
FOR CONTENTMENT

I have learned the secret of being content in any and every situation, whether well fed or hungry, whether living in plenty or in want.

PHILIPPIANS 4:12

If you are to know contentment—that quietness of heart, supernaturally given, that gladly submits to God in all circumstances—you must undergo a learning process.

When I learned to feed myself in the hospital, I felt like giving up many times. Wearing a bib, smearing applesauce all over my clothes, and having it land more times on my lap than in my mouth was humiliating.

I had to make a series of difficult choices. Was I going to let disappointing failures overwhelm me? I'm convinced God gave me the strength to lift that spoon to my mouth, and today I manage a spoon quite well.

Contentment has to be learned. And it requires strength from beyond this world. But once you gain it, though you have nothing, you will have everything. There is great joy in that![283]

JONI EARECKSON TADA

Heavenly Father, help me learn how to become
content and at peace. As you strengthen me,
help me to do everything I need to do. Amen.

MONDAY

PERSPECTIVE IS EVERYTHING

I will rejoice in the LORD,
I will be joyful in God my Savior.

HABAKKUK 3:18

Since I travel most weekends, Monday is the day I unpack. That's always a mess, with stuff everywhere. Then there's the laundry … piles of clothes that need washing. I have this theory that after the Lord comes and time is no more, somewhere, in a remote corner of the world, dirty laundry will still be waiting.

On Monday I must make stops at the grocery store, the cleaners, the bank, the post office, the service station, the hairdresser. Mondays annoy me.

But in another way, I love Mondays. I love unloading all my stuff out of the suitcase and organizing it back where it belongs. I love pulling fresh laundry from the dryer and folding it while it's still warm.

On Monday nights, I feel genuine joy, having such a sense of accomplishment. Why do I sometimes get bogged down with chores, hating the day? Then, at other times, I get fired up with enthusiasm, loving the day? Perspective! Perspective is everything. The busiest days can become our most joyful.[284]

LUCI SWINDOLL

TUESDAY

I'm Joy-Happy

May those who do what is right be glad
and filled with joy when they are with him.
May they be happy and joyful.

PSALM 68:3 NIRV

We're often taught to be careful of the difference between joy and happiness. Happiness, it is said, is an emotion that depends upon what "happens." Joy, by contrast, is supposed to be enduring, stemming from deep within our souls and not affected by the circumstances surrounding us.

It's an appropriate linguistic distinction, I suppose. But I don't think God had any such hairsplitting in mind. Scripture uses the terms interchangeably, along with words like *delight*, *gladness*, *blessed*. There is no scale of relative spiritual values applied to any of these. Happiness is not relegated to flesh-minded sinners, nor joy to heaven-bound saints.

To rob joy of its elated twin, happiness, is to deprive our soul of God's feast. Seek both as part and parcel in all circumstances. When your soul is stirred by a deep contentment, be happy. When a delightful moment strikes that is quite outside yourself, be joyful. Accept them both as a gift from a God who is rich in all such emotions.[285]

JONI EARECKSON TADA

WEDNESDAY

✿

RESPITE FOR YOUR SOUL

The LORD says,
"I will refresh the weary and satisfy the faint."

JEREMIAH 31:25

As a child I was thrilled when the bookmobile rolled into my area. I would eagerly pedal a little more than a mile to get to it. Happily fortified with new reading selections, I'd pedal back home, clambor up the makeshift ladder to my tree house, and settle in.

When was the last time you settled in for a mindlessly pleasant read? Why don't you do that more often? What's driving you continually to be productive?

Perhaps you, like me, are missing out on recreational activity that has no purpose other than to give a needed respite from our task-oriented lives. Wouldn't it be fun occasionally to produce nothing, accomplish nothing, and contribute to nothing? Maybe that means reading a book that doesn't require a pen; maybe it's a cup of something at a coffee house, or maybe it's a meander through the mall or a stroll (not a jog) through the park. The possibilities for nothing are endless.[286] Make it a date and recharge your joy.

MARILYN MEBERG

THURSDAY

✾

THE JOY OF THE ANGELS

Suddenly a great company of the heavenly host
appeared with the angel, praising God and saying,
"Glory to God in the highest,
and on earth peace to men on whom his favor rests."

LUKE 2:13–14

The night skies over Bethlehem were cool and quiet; and then suddenly the veil of heaven parted for an instant, and an angel stepped through the curtain of night.

Not long ago I decided to paint this scene. But I needed someone to model as an angel. I called my secretary into the art studio and asked her to stand on a chair and drape a sheet around herself. "Now," I said, "think of your happiest memory!" She rubbed her chin and then an idea dawned. Throwing back her head, she hollered, "Whoopee!" I quickly sketched the joy in her face. In no time I had my angel on the canvas.

Most of us think of the word *rejoice* when we remember that amazing scene. Smile when you say it…see it…sing it…or read about it in the Scriptures. After all, the announcement of the angels was alive, active, and *full* of joy![287]

JONI EARECKSON TADA

FRIDAY

FILL UP YOUR SENSES WITH HIM

O taste and see that the LORD is good;
happy are those who take refuge in him.

PSALM 34:8 NRSV

Two young children were playing a game they called "God is …" They took turns finishing the sentence with positive descriptions of God. Six-year-old Missy finally ventured, "God smells good all the time. Sometimes he smells like orange blossoms. Tonight he smells like strawberries."

Maybe Missy was really just enjoying the smell of the strawberry bubble bath. But maybe she can lead us to a new appreciation of a spiritual metaphor. In 2 Corinthians 2:15, Paul says that we believers are "the aroma of Christ."

God wants to use you to spread the aroma of Christ. Are you able to joy in that metaphor? Can you inhale a little deeper and longer to enjoy the fragrance yourself?

Stop the rat race. Enjoy the rich aromas in your life—the ones God gives in nature and the ones God gives through the witness of human kindness. Stop and enjoy the sights, tastes, and smells of God's good gifts.[288] Let his joy fill you to overflowing.

SHEILA WALSH

WEEKEND

THE APPLE OF HIS EYE

Whoever touches you touches the apple of his eye.

ZECHARIAH 2:8

Who's the apple of your eye? Whoever it is, one thing is certain—you love that individual with a fervent and intense love. That person gives you joy indescribable.

You are the apple of God's eye. God feels powerful emotions when it comes to you. His joy is not merely satisfaction over something you do, as though you had him wrapped around your little finger with that winsome way of yours. God's joy is in his own goodness and wisdom, in the beautiful character of his Son, and in the complexity and wonder of all that he has made. His joy is in who he has created you to be.[289]

JONI EARECKSON TADA

*Help me to remember, Lord, that your joy over me
is pure and perfect and rooted in the way you love your
Son. I can hardly believe that you actually feel
something deep, powerful, and joyful when it comes
to me—and it's all because of Jesus. Thank you
for making me the apple of your eye.[287] Amen.*

MONDAY

OFFER AN UPLIFTING WORD

The Sovereign LORD has taught me what to say,
so that I can strengthen the weary.

ISAIAH 50:4 GNT

I sometimes feel as if I've given all I can. Whatever project it is, I fling it out to the world…and then it comes back to me, bearing strength and joy in the words of women (and men, too) from all over the globe. Proverbs 17:22 says, "A cheerful heart is good medicine," and that's the tonic I receive when I read these uplifting messages.

Of course, my mail includes letters filled with hurt and pain, too—the heartfelt cries of parents who have lost a child through death or alienation. But the joyful letters give me the strength to encourage those parents as I realize that many of them once wrote with the same devastating heartache as the "new" parents are expressing. And now, here they are, able to smile once more and even share a little laughter. They have seen God turn their grief into joy—and that has become their strength. Who do you know who could use an uplifting word today?[290]

BARBARA JOHNSON

TUESDAY

SECOND CHANCES

Love keeps no record of wrongs.

1 CORINTHIANS 13:5

I walked into a bank to meet with an executive vice-president about customer-service training. I went up to the secretary's desk, smiled, and announced my name and my reason for being there. The secretary stopped working, looked me up and down, and walked off, leaving me standing there. She had decided I wasn't worth a nod, let alone a smile or a handshake.

When I taught the customer-service class, she was a top participant—pleasant, positive, polite, and poised. But her lasting impression remained my first impression of her. I wasn't following Christ's admonition to give people room to make a second impression. I needed to give her a second chance.

Maybe you have written off someone. That person just might deserve a second chance.

God knows us inside out and outside in. He understands what motivates us and accepts us even in our worst moments. I want to be able to do the same for others.[291] Without second chances, there can be little joy.

THELMA WELLS

WEDNESDAY

❋

A BANQUET FOR ALL

Join me in giving glory to the LORD.
  Let us honor him together.

PSALM 34:3 NIRV

The pleasures of God are never private pleasures. They are, as Dr. John Piper says, "always shared, public, and communal." The joy we experience in our salvation is true, radiant, and sincere only when we share it with others.

The apostle Paul served many a banquet plate up to others, calling them "my joy and crown" (Philippians 4:1). The apostle John doubled his joy whenever he brought someone new to the Good News table. My motive in writing is the desire to double my joy by passing the plate of God's blessings to as many people as I can.

The banquet of God's blessings will taste sweeter if you invite someone to take a seat next to you. What aspect of the gospel can you share with someone today? Ask God to show you people who are hungry for the things of God. Then pass the platter…and experience the joy![292]

JONI EARECKSON TADA

THURSDAY

❋

JESUS *IS* JOY

Jesus said, "If you obey my commands, you will remain in my love, just as I have obeyed my Father's commands and remain in his love. I have told you this so that my joy may be in you and that your joy may be complete."

JOHN 15:10–11

There's really no easy formula for appropriating joy. Joy happens in us as God restores us, teaching us to abide in him as he works in and through us.

Joy is not something that you can buy. You can't get it from a book or a conference. You can't absorb it by hanging out with people who seem to have it. You can spend your life trying to eliminate all pain and stress in the vain hope that joy will take its place, but it won't. Joy comes only when you live in relationship with the source of joy.

Remember John 15:4? "Remain in me, and I will remain in you. No branch can bear fruit by itself; it must remain in the vine. Neither can you bear fruit unless you remain in me." You can't go out and work on joy. We are called to rest in the One who *is* joy. Without him there is no joy.[293]

SHEILA WALSH

FRIDAY

COMMUNING WITH OUR GOD

You will call upon me and come and pray to me,
and I will listen to you.

JEREMIAH 29:12

We can express our prayers in volumes of beautiful words praising God for the glorious sunrise and sunset, for magnificent roses in full bloom, for the miracle of a newborn's birth, or for the love of a friend or family member. We can commune with God using eloquent phrases and long praising prayers. We an confess our wrongdoings by talking with him in detail for hours, days, months, asking for the Holy Spirit's guidance and strength in our daily endeavors. We can come to him with appreciative words eloquent and vast, with lengthy poems of thanksgiving for his abundant generosity. And we can sit quietly with our Father for long stretches of time, never saying a word, but communing with him in spirit. Prayers need not be long, but neither must they be brief.

Surely, our Father offers us so many ways to express our desires, thoughts, and dreams to him. Prayer can help us live more closely to God, to dwell in his presence, and to nourish ourselves with his word. Have you rejoiced in your Lord?[294]

DENISE GEORGE

WEEKEND

IT'S AN ATTITUDE THING

From the ends of the earth I call to you,
I call as my heart grows faint;
lead me to the rock that is higher than I.

PSALM 61:2

We need to recognize the vast difference between mere inconvenience and a major catastrophe. Nobody ever said life would be easy or without problems. Everyone knows that. The secret to handling problems is in how we view them. It's an attitude thing. Running out of coffee is inconvenient. A rained-out picnic is inconvenient. But a smashed jaw, broken cheekbone, crushed nose, and missing eye? Now we're talking catastrophe!

I think life is to be experienced joyfully rather than endured grudgingly. We know it brings complexities and trouble. Scripture affirms that. But why do we take minor irritations so seriously? Think of the pain and conflict we would spare ourselves, the stress we would forego, if we just realized that mere inconveniences can be survived.[295]

LUCI SWINDOLL

Heavenly Father, when I can't see the forest for the trees,
lead me up to the place where you are so that
I may gain your perspective. Amen.

MONDAY

✦

ANIXIETY CAN
THROTTLE YOUR JOY

Anxiety weighs down the human heart,
  but a good word cheers it up.

PROVERBS 12:25 NRSV

I have a bit of a "germ-thing." So I was eating my entire meal at a cafeteria with an oversized spoon I had found in an obscure container slightly behind the soft ice-cream machine.

"How long have you had this germ thing?" Luci asked.

"Since the sixth grade," I replied. "Our science teacher had us touch some specially treated sponge, and overnight it grew bacteria cultures that we watched develop into various horrifying configurations. I've never been the same since."

Luci slowly put down her fork and studied it for a second. Then, with renewed enthusiasm, she announced, "If those germs haven't gotten me by this time in my life, I don't think they ever will!"

Her healthy response reminded me that for me to fear the unseen and worry about its potential to do harm throttles my joy. Of course, one should observe hygienic health practices, but if carried to an extreme, they can lead to wrestling with a too-large spoon in a cafeteria with plenty of right-sized forks.[296]

MARILYN MEBERG

TUESDAY

TRUST AND TAKE ONE MORE STEP

When I am afraid,
I will trust in you.
In God, whose word I praise,
in God I trust; I will not be afraid.

PSALM 56:3–4

When I was eighteen, my favorite book was *Hinds Feet on High Places* by Hannah Hunnard. It tells the story of a young girl named Much Afraid, who chooses to leave the valley of fear where she has lived and follow the shepherd up into the mountain. Time after time, she wants to stop and go back to the valley because the road ahead looks all wrong.

At every key point when Much Afraid chooses to trust the shepherd and take one more step, the shepherd gives her a stone to keep. At the end of her long journey, when she finally "dies to herself" and is given new legs with which to run, she is taken to the top of the mountain. There she sees that each rough, colorless stone had become a beautiful jewel for her crown.

I believe that God would have us live trusting him at every turn. There is no other way to live,[297] if we are going to truly experience the joy of the Lord.

SHEILA WALSH

WEDNESDAY

BE HOLY

It is written:
"Be holy, because I am holy."

1 PETER 1:16

When the Holy Spirit awakens the heart of a person to delight in the holiness of God, an urgent and aching desire is born, not only to behold that holiness, as from a distance, but also to be holy as God is holy. Your joy will never be complete as long as you are standing outside looking in.

Don't just see the grace of God from a distance; share in the power of that grace. Feel him delivering you, helping you conquer temptation in your life. Feel God's grace coursing through you to save others. Why? Because once you begin to participate in his life, the more you will want to feel. The more you experience, the more you will want to experience. The more you desire to feel, see, experience, and know God, the more you will be inclined to right living—pride conquered, temper subdued, selfishness skewered. Behold the holiness of God and you *will* be holy, and your joy will be complete.[298]

JONI EARECKSON TADA

THURSDAY

AN ALTITUDE ADJUSTMENT

I will praise God's name in song
  and glorify him with thanksgiving.
This will please the LORD.

PSALM 69:30–31

I wasn't all that thrilled about flying. Yet one day I realized that navigating the airways was to be a constant part of my life, and I was going to lose my joy a lot if I didn't make some altitude adjustments. I needed another perspective. So I put on a gratitude attitude before boarding because:

    1. It provides a way to travel that allows me to dart about the country and do things I could never do otherwise.

    2. I might be able to offer a word of kindness to an anxious traveler or a stressed flight attendant.

    3. As unskilled at cooking as I am, I can still offer up a better meal than the airlines!

    Maybe you find yourself taxiing around your home or office with a jet-sized 'tude. Try sitting still and ask the Lord for a fresh perspective for an old routine. Then prepare for take-off and enjoy the amazing view.[299]

PATSY CLAIRMONT

FRIDAY

A GIFT OF WHATEVER YOU HAVE

Jesus said, "Give, and it will be given to you.
A good measure, pressed down, shaken together
and running over, will be poured into your lap.
For with the measure you use, it will be measured to you."

LUKE 6:38

Charles Darrow didn't set out to become a millionaire when he developed "Monopoly," the game by Parker Brothers, but that's what happened. The little gift he developed from scraps of cardboard and tiny pieces of wood was simply a way to keep his wife's spirits up during her Depression-era pregnancy; ultimately, that gift came back to him as bountiful riches.

Are times tough in your little apartment—or lavish mansion? If it seems as if your world is collapsing around you and you feel yourself slipping into the depths of depression, don't despair. Your attitude can set the tone for your whole family. So use whatever scraps you can find—even if, in the beginning, it's just a scrap of a smile—and make a gift of whatever you have. Then watch the gifts come back to you[300] and fill your home with joy.

BARBARA JOHNSON

WEEKEND

YOU CAN DEPEND ON HIS LOVE

*Jesus said, "As the Father has loved me, so have I
loved you. Now remain in my love."*

JOHN 15:9

D o you enjoy hearing those tender words, "I love you,"
from your spouse, children, family, and friends? Of
course, you do. However, to know that we are loved by an
omnipotent, omnipresent, omniscient Lord is the grandest
feeling of acceptance anyone can have. When other people fail
to express their love to us, we can always depend on Jesus.

Imagine Jesus saying to you, "Child of mine, I love you
with an everlasting love. I love you with unconditional love. I
love because I want to! I love you when others think you are
unlovable. I love you when you have sinned and come short of
my glory. I love you in the good times and in the bad."[301] Let
it fill your heart with joy.

THELMA WELLS

> *Heavenly Father, it boggles my mind that you love me so
> unconditionally. Your love far surpasses the love any
> human can have for me, and it comforts me and fills me
> with joy as I allow myself to bask in it. Amen.*

MONDAY

✦

JUST BE YOURSELF

Enter his gates with thanksgiving
  and his courts with praise;
  give thanks to him and praise his name.

PSALM 100:4

The Scottish writer George MacDonald said, "It is the heart that is not yet sure of its God that is afraid to laugh in his presence."

So often with old people and children, all sense of what would be appropriate is swallowed up in what feels right. That's refreshing. We waste too many years between childhood and our older years measuring our behavior on a scale we think we see in someone else's eyes.

God loves us as we are right now! I love the freedom to be myself in God. I pray that a year from now I will be a more godly woman, but I know God won't love me any more than he does right this minute.

Do you find yourself coming into God's presence wondering what kind of reception you'll get? Let me tell you, you can run in out of the cold, sit by the fire, put up your feet, and just be yourself. You are loved.[302] That's something to rejoice about!

SHEILA WALSH

TUESDAY

THE REALITY OF HEAVEN

He that hath an ear, let him hear what the Spirit saith unto the churches; To him that overcometh will I give to eat of the hidden manna.

At present, abstract things like truth and goodness have no substance. Oh, we see these qualities manifested in others, but they are not concrete in themselves. In heaven, though, purity and goodness, righteousness and joy will have more substance than anything we ever touched, tasted, or smelled on earth. We are wrong in thinking heaven is wispy and vaporous. It is earth that is like withering grass, not heaven.

One day we will *eat* of the hidden manna. We will *wear* righteousness like light. We will *shine* like the stars in the universe. We shall *eat* from the Tree of Life. *Hold* the Morning Star like a scepter. *Enter* into the joy of the Lord. There is nothing vague or wispy about these verbs. Everything in heaven will have more substance than we ever dreamed. The question for you today is this: Are you ready for the real reality? You can be. [303]

JONI EARECKSON TADA

WEDNESDAY

✦

WARMING HEARTS

If two lie down together, they will keep warm.
    But how can one keep warm alone?
Though one may be overpowered,
    two can defend themselves.
A cord of three strands is not quickly broken.

ECCLESIASTES 4:11–12

A cold day. It swirls snow, kicking up a storm. It takes something extra to stick to the job, keep your kids happy in the house, get to church, and be a good neighbor in those frosty winter months.

We experience frigid temperatures in our faith, too, when hope dies: love walks out the door, a friend moves out of town, the job ends, the bank fails. God seems distant. Prayer fades in your throat before you barely utter a word. The Bible stares back with a blank page. You might call it spiritual frostbite.

The church is God's spiritual stove. In its containment, we pile on fuel, stir the embers, strike a match. We need each other's warmth to survive the winters of our lives. Who needs a hand, a word, or one of your ears for a few moments? Reach out and warm a heart![304] It will bring joy to your soul.

BARBARA JOHNSON

THURSDAY

✺

ACCEPTABLE PRAISE

Sing joyfully to the LORD, you righteous;
it is fitting for the upright to praise him.

PSALM 33:1

Have you ever watched an infant caress his mother? He "goos" and "gaahs," slobbering his affection all over her cheek. He laughs in her arms, breaks into a squeal, and spits a "brrrrh!" of curdled milk into her face. In a bumbling attempt to reach for his mother's chin, he might even slap her neck.

If you chided that infant, you might get a sock in the jaw from his mother. That infant is his mother's joy, no matter how awkward it may come across.

God is the same way. Some of us are babes in the Lord, but praise is becoming, even from a baby. Some believers start off well praising God but get sidetracked into listing petitions. Others seem to run out of words to say or fear they are saying the wrong words. They give up too easily.

Don't get down on yourself if your praises don't seem to measure up. Like an infant's affections to his parent, they *will* be pleasing to the Lord.[305]

JONI EARECKSON TADA

FRIDAY

ONE TRUE HAPPINESS

Therefore my heart is glad and my tongue rejoices; my body also will live in hope.

ACTS 2:26

There is only one happiness for created human spirits. God made our hearts for himself. They cannot rest until they rest in Him. It is true that while the world smiles upon us with all the conveniences and luxuries of life, we frequently enjoy a kind of happiness, but we still pant after something else. That *something* is neither more nor less than the knowledge and love of God as manifested in the Son of His love, through the eternal Spirit.

If you are now unhappy, it is because you have taken a wrong way to a right end. You have been seeking happiness where it never was and never can be found—in your fellow creatures, instead of your Creator.

You can find the happiness you seek in the union of your spirit with the Father of spirits. You can find it in the knowledge and love of God who is the fountain of happiness.[306]

JOHN WESLEY

WEEKEND

❖

MAN OF SORROWS... LORD OF JOY

Jesus said, "I say these things while I am still in the world, so that they may have the full measure of my joy within them."

JOHN 17:13

According to 2 Corinthians 6:10, we mortals are "sorrowful, yet always rejoicing." A father stands at the altar and sighs deeply as he gives his daughter's hand in marriage. A mother watches her son languish behind prison bars but sees the experience bring the rebellious young man to repentance. This is understandable for humans, but how can God be sorrowful, yet always rejoicing?

Isaiah called Jesus a man of sorrows, and yet, he is also described as the "Lord of joy." This may be because, as the Son of God, he sees enough of the coming ecstasy to make up for the present agony. And God sees this glorious end as clearly as if it were today. God can be truly and utterly happy and yet filled with grief.

JONI EARECKSON TADA

*Lord, help me to learn to live in you today
so I may see the coming ecstasy and realize it
makes up for my present hurt and heartache.
Help me to be rejoicing while I am sorrowful.[307] Amen.*

MONDAY

❋

DO WE MATTER?

The LORD says,
"See I have engraved you on the palms of my hands."

ISAIAH 49:16

The holiday we celebrate as Christmas memorializes God's answer to the question, *Do we matter?* Here on earth, for thirty-three years, God experienced in flesh what it is like to be one of us. In the stories he told, and the people whose lives he touched, Jesus answered for all time that vexing question.

Jesus said, God is like a shepherd who leaves ninety-nine sheep inside the fence to hunt frantically for one stray; he is like a father who can't stop thinking about his rebellious ingrate of a child, though he has another who is respectful and obedient. God loves people not as a race or species, but rather just as you and I love them: one at a time. We *matter* to God. In a rare moment when he pulled back the curtain between the seen and unseen worlds, Jesus said that angels rejoice when a single sinner repents. A solitary act on this speck of a planet reverberates throughout the cosmos.[308]

PHILIP YANCEY

TUESDAY

THE PERFECT BALANCE

Water will gush forth in the wilderness
and streams in the desert.
The burning sand will become a pool,
the thirsty ground bubbling springs.

ISAIAH 35:6–7

One of the things I find fascinating about God's creation is the way he seems to temper the negative environmental elements with corresponding positive ones. For instance, without the nearly ceaseless rains of the Northwest, no incomparable green scenery would greet the eye from all directions. And the snow that snuggles over Mount Hood, Mount Rainier, and Mount Saint Helens would not exist if, at lower elevations, there were no rain.

By the same token, if God had not created water for the desert environment, it would indeed be an ashtray. But because of water, we have luxuriously green golf courses, languidly swaying palm trees, and even streams in the desert.

God's creative style ensures that something wonderful will offset something less than wonderful. In everything God seems so balanced. I love that about him.[309] It makes my heart glad.

MARILYN MEBERG

WEDNESDAY

❁

"Ooh!...Ah!"

The heavens declare the glory of God;
the skies proclaim the work of his hands.

PSALM 19:1

God is a giver. His generosity is obvious in how lavishly he bestows on us rainbows, waterfalls, canyons, and white caps.

One day when I was visiting in the desert, a marshmallow cloud formation drizzled over the mountaintop like whipped cream. I brought my bike to a standstill and just beheld this delicious scene. Another evening the sunset turned the skyline into a saucer of peaches and cream—absolutely dreamy. The Lord serves up his scrumptious beauty in liberal portions and then invites us to partake.

I have often joined Marilyn Meberg at nightfall for the spectacular performance as the sun sets. The mountains go through a series of thrilling changes. From pinks to lavenders to deep purples, the setting sun and emerging evening appear to cover the hillside for sleep. Marilyn and I never tire of the Lord's thrilling displays. We "ooh!" and "ah!" and can feel our blood pressure balancing out as smiles and giggles help us to express our gratitude.[310] The joy of the Lord abounds.

PATSY CLAIRMONT

THURSDAY

JESUS IS MY FLASHLIGHT

The LORD says,
"I will turn the darkness into light before them
  and make the rough places smooth.
These are the things I will do;
  I will not forsake them."

ISAIAH 42:16

My bus driver's name on this particular tour was "Shooter." One day on the road, I was waiting in the lobby for a cab to take me to the nearest drugstore. Shooter also happened to be there.

Out of the blue, he said to me, "Kathy, you get up in the morning with a good attitude. I like that."

Nowhere near every morning, I thought. But I was thankful for his observation.

"This is how I look at it," he said. "The sun comes up every morning, and I'm grateful for another day to be alive. And you know what? If the sun never came up, we could all use a flashlight."

Shooter's words touched me deeply that day. I am a believer in Jesus and his promises. If the sun doesn't shine, I do indeed have a flashlight: His Word is a lamp unto my feet, guiding my every step. The sweet glow of his presence shines into my darkness.[311] His light fills me with joy.

KATHY TROCCOLI

FRIDAY

SMART MONEY

Jesus said, "Whoever can be trusted with very little
can also be trusted with much, and whoever is dishonest
with very little will also be dishonest with much.
So if you have not been trustworthy in handling
worldly wealth, who will trust you with true riches?"

LUKE 16:10–11

I follow simple but practical principles about handling money. These guidelines help me make wise financial choices and control my money without it controlling me. Consider these joyful financial tips: 1) Tithe off your gross income; 2) Live within your means; 3) Wear things out; 4) Do it yourself; 5) Anticipate your needs; 6) Consider multiple uses for things; 7) Make gifts; 8) Shop less; 9) Buy used; 10) Pay cash; 11) Try doing without.

Let me give you three other suggestions that I find helpful: First, if the pleasure of having something is sweeter to you than the pain of paying it off, don't be afraid of indebtedness. But you must manage it. Second, don't compare what you have with what others have. Third, if you want to be the happiest person in town, give away more than you keep. No matter how little money is in your purse, you're already rich.[312]

LUCI SWINDOLL

WEEKEND

❋

TAKE YOUR RAINBOW WITH YOU

We are hard pressed on every side, but not crushed;
perplexed, but not in despair; persecuted, but not
abandoned; struck down, but not destroyed.

2 CORINTHIANS 4:8–9

God washes us and cleans us up. His love rinses away the residue we pick up trying to protect ourselves from life's scratchy circumstances. When he is finished with us, we are shining, transparent, lustrous.

Certainly the rain falls on the just and the unjust (chiefly on the just, because the unjust steal their umbrellas). But a few splashes of pain don't get me down for long. In the cesspools of life, I remember the colorful splashes of joy. I take my rainbow with me and share it with others!

We cannot protect ourselves from trouble, but we can dance through the puddles of life with a rainbow smile, twirling the only umbrella we need—the umbrella of God's love. His covering of grace is sufficient for any problem we may have.[313] His joy will be your constant source of strength.

BARBARA JOHNSON

Heavenly Father, infuse me with your grace and
help me to stand on your promises so that I may
endure joyfully and come out on top. Amen.

[1] Andrew Murray, *With Christ in the School of Prayer*, "Third Lesson," (New York City, NY: Fleming H. Revell Company, 1895).

[2] Patsy Clairmont, Barbara Johnson, Marilyn Meberg, Luci Swindoll, Sheila Walsh, Thelma Wells, *Overjoyed!* (Grand Rapids, Mich.: Zondervan, 1999).

[3] Kathy Troccoli, *My Life Is in Your Hands* (Grand Rapids, Mich.: Zondervan, 1997).

[4] Patsy Clairmont, Barbara Johnson, Marilyn Meberg, Luci Swindoll, Sheila Walsh, and Thelma Wells, *We Brake for Joy!* (Grand Rapids, Mich.: Zondervan, 1998).

[5] Joni Eareckson Tada, *More Precious Than Silver* (Grand Rapids, Mich.: Zondervan, 1998).

[6] Patsy Clairmont, Barbara Johnson, Marilyn Meberg, and Luci Swindoll, *Joy Breaks* (Grand Rapids, Mich.: Zondervan, 1997).

[7] Jodi Berndt, *Praying the Scriptures for Your Children* (Grand Rapids, Mich.: Zondervan, 2001).

[8] Philip D. Yancey, *The Bible Jesus Read* (Grand Rapids, Mich.: Zondervan, 1999).

[9] Traci Mullins, *Finding Joy* (Grand Rapids, Mich.: Zondervan, 1998), 13–14.

[10] *Joy for a Woman's Soul: Promises to Refresh Your Spirit* (Grand Rapids, Mich.: Zondervan, 1998), 171.

[11] Ibid., 184.

[12] Sheila Walsh, *Bring Back the Joy* (Grand Rapids, Mich.: Zondervan, 1998).

[13] Troccoli, 15.

[14] Richard Carlson, Ph.D., *Don't Sweat the Small Stuff...and it's all small stuff* (city needed: Hyperion, 1997), 1–2.

[15] Mullins, 23–24.

[16] Joni Eareckson Tada, *Diamonds in the Dust* (Grand Rapids, Mich.: Zondervan, 1993), May 20.

[17] *Joy for a Woman's Soul*, 80.

[18] Ibid., 94.

[19] Barbara Johnson, *Boomerang Joy* (Grand Rapids, Mich.: Zondervan, 1998).

[20] *Joy for a Woman's Soul*, 183.

[21] Ibid., 187.

[22] Tada, *More Precious Than Silver*, September 26.

[23] *Joy for a Woman's Soul*, 122.

[24] Troccoli, 19.

[25] *Joy for a Woman's Soul*, 83.

[26] Mullins, 51–52.

[27] *Joy for a Woman's Soul*, 95.

[28] Ibid., 169.

[29] Ibid., 186.

[30] Sheila Walsh, *Honestly* (Grand Rapids, Mich.:

Zondervan, 1996), 47.

[31] *Joy for a Woman's Soul*, 79.

[32] Yancey, 36.

[33] Clairmont, Johnson, Meberg, Swindoll, 98–99.

[34] Troccoli, 22.

[35] Clairmont, Johnson, Meberg, Swindoll, 104–105.

[36] Ibid., 116–117.

[37] Mullins, 61.

[38] *Joy for a Woman's Soul*, 153.

[39] Clairmont, Johnson, Meberg, Swindoll, Walsh, Wells *Overjoyed!* 128.

[40] Walsh, *Honestly*, 73.

[41] *Joy for a Woman's Soul*, 82.

[42] Yancey, 126.

[43] Clairmont, Johnson, Meberg, Swindoll.

[44] Walsh, *Honestly*, 59.

[45] Troccoli, 30–31.

[46] Clairmont, Johnson, Meberg, Swindoll, 128.

[47] *Joy for a Woman's Soul*, 180.

[48] Clairmont, Johnson, Meberg, Swindoll, 150–151.

[49] Tada, *Diamonds in the Dust*, February 10.

[50] Walsh, *Honestly*, 73–74.

[51] *Joy for a Woman's Soul*, 130.

[52] Yancey, 194.

[53] *Joy for a Woman's Soul*, 128.

[54] Patsy Clairmont, Barbara Johnson, Marilyn Meberg, Luci Swindoll, *The Joyful Journey* (Grand Rapids, Mich.: Zondervan, 1997), 33.

[55] Troccoli, 43.

[56] *Joy for a Woman's Soul*, 65.

[57] Clairmont, Johnson, Meberg, Swindoll, Walsh, Wells, *Overjoyed!* 146.

[58] *Joy for a Woman's Soul*, 71.

[59] Tada, *More Precious Than Silver*, September 30.

[60] Clairmnt, Johnson, Meberg, Swindoll, *Joy Breaks!* 155–156.

[61] C. S. Lewis, *Reflections on the Psalms*, 95. [There is no publisher info in this footnote. Is that okay?]

[62] Tada, *More Precious Than Silver*, March 11.

[63] *Joy for a Woman's Soul*, 12.

[64] Tada, *More Precious Than Silver*, March 19.

[65] *Joy for a Woman's Soul*, 131.

[66] Troccoli, 53–54.

[67] *Joy for a Woman's Soul*, 68.

[68] Tada, *More Precious Than Silver*, November 7.

[69] *Joy for a Woman's Soul*, 74.

[70] Walsh, *Honestly*, 96.

[71] *Joy for a Woman's Soul*, 9.

[72] Clairmont, Johnson, Meberg, Swindoll, *Joy Breaks!* 174–175.

[73] Yancey, 215–216.
[74] Tada, *More Precious Than Silver*, June 14.
[75] Clairmont, Johnson, Meberg, Swindoll, *Joy Breaks!* 78–79.
[76] Troccoli, 39.
[77] Clairmont, Johnson, Meberg, Swindoll, *Joy Breaks!* 95.
[78] New Life Clinics, *Laughter for a Woman's Soul* (Grand Rapids, Mich.: Zondervan, 2001), 100.
[79] Ibid., 157.
[80] Tada, *More Precious Than Silver*, June 14.
[81] Walsh, *Honestly*, 101.
[82] Clairmont, Johnson, Meberg, Swindoll, *Joy Breaks!* 182.
[83] Tada, *Diamonds in the Dust*, January 5.
[84] Women of Faith, Inc., *Experiencing God's Presence* (Grand Rapids, Mich.: Zondervan, 1998), 35.
[85] Clairmont, Johnson, Meberg, Swindoll, *Joy Breaks!* 131.
[86] Troccoli, 137–138.
[87] Walsh, *Bring Back the Joy*, 58, 60.
[88] Tada, *Diamonds in the Dust*, January 8.
[89] New Life Clinics, 85.
[90] Tada, *Diamonds in the Dust*, May 31.
[91] Ibid., January 20.
[92] Walsh, *Honestly*, 118.
[93] Denise George, *Tilling the Soul*, (Grand Rapids, Mich.: Zondervan, 2004), 85–86.
[94] Tada, *Diamonds in the Dust*, February 24.
[95] Clairmont, Johnson, Meberg, Swindoll, *Joy Breaks!* 147–148.
[96] Troccoli, 62, 64.
[97] New Life Clinics, 107.
[98] *Women's Devotional Bible 2* (Grand Rapids, Mich.: Zondervan, 1995), 519.
[99] New Life Clinics, 17.
[100] Judith Couchman, *Shaping a Woman's Soul* (Grand Rapids, Mich.: Zondervan, 1996), 29.
[101] Patsy Clairmont, Barbara Johnson, Marilyn Meberg, Luci Swindoll, *The Joyful Journey* (Grand Rapids, Mich.: Zondervan, 1997), 43.
[102] *Joy for a Woman's Soul*, 76.
[103] New Life Clinics, 142.
[104] Walsh, *Honestly*, 121.
[105] Tada, *Diamonds in the Dust*, January 24.
[106] Troccoli, 78–79.
[107] Tada, *Diamonds in the Dust*, June 29.
[108] Patsy Clairmont, Barbara Johnson, Marilyn Meberg, Luci Swindoll, Sheila Walsh, Thelma Wells *Outrageous Joy* (Grand Rapids, Mich.: Zondervan, 1999), 84–85.
[109] Tada, *Diamonds in the Dust*, February 8.
[110] Walsh, *Honestly*, 81–82.
[111] New Life Clinics, 12.

[112] Gloria Gaither, Sue Buchanan, Peggy Benson, Joy MacKenzie, *Friends through Thick & Thin* (Grand Rapids, Mich.: Zondervan, 1998), 55.
[113] Tada, *Diamonds in the Dust*, July 3.
[114] Walsh, *Honestly*, 177.
[115] Tada, *Diamonds in the Dust*, February 10.
[116] Tada, *More Precious Than Silver*, June 17.
[117] Troccoli, 82–83.
[118] *Joy for a Woman's Soul*, 64.
[119] *Peace for a Woman's Soul* (Grand Rapids, Mich.: Zondervan, 2002), 113.
[120] Walsh, *Honestly*, 122.
[121] Tada, *Diamonds in the Dust*, February 22.
[122] *Peace for a Woman's Soul*, 203.
[123] Tada, *Diamonds in the Dust*, July 15.
[124] *NIV Women of Faith Study Bible, New International Version* (Grand Rapids, Mich.: Zondervan, 2001).
[125] Tada, *Diamonds in the Dust*, July 29.
[126] *Joy for a Woman's Soul*, 201.
[127] Tada, *Diamonds in the Dust*, March 24.
[128] Troccoli, 83.
[129] *Peace for a Woman's Soul*, 114.
[130] Walsh, *Honestly*, 178–179.
[131] Tada, *Diamonds in the Dust*, August 23.
[132] *Peace for a Woman's Soul*, 81.
[133] Tada, *Diamonds in the Dust*, April 3.
[134] *Peace for a Woman's Soul*, 155.
[135] *Joy for a Woman's Soul*, 166.
[136] Ibid., 199.
[137] Troccoli, 86–87.
[138] Tada, *Diamonds in the Dust*, August 27.
[139] *Peace for a Woman's Soul*, 23.
[140] Tada, *More Precious Than Silver*, July 14.
[141] Walsh, *Honestly*, 185–187.
[142] *Joy for a Woman's Soul*, 55.
[143] *NIV Women of Faith Study Bible, New International Version*.
[144] *Joy for a Woman's Soul*, 53.
[145] Ibid., 178.
[146] Ibid., 204.
[147] Troccoli, 109.
[148] Tada, *Diamonds in the Dust*, April 4.
[149] *Joy for a Woman's Soul*, 52.
[150] Ibid., 157.
[151] Sheila Walsh, *Living Fearlessly* (Grand Rapids, Mich.: Zondervan, 2001), 14–15.
[152] Tada, *More Precious Than Silver*, August 18.
[153] Tada, *Diamonds in the Dust*, April 8.
[154] Walsh, *Bring Back the Joy*, 43.
[155] Tada, *Diamonds in the Dust*, September 4.
[156] *Peace for a Woman's Soul*, 21.
[157] *Joy for a Woman's Soul*, 175.
[158] Troccoli, 147.

159 *Joy for a Woman's Soul*, 21.

160 *Peace for a Woman's Soul*, 57.

161 Walsh, *Living Fearlessly*, 12, 34.

162 George, *Tilling the Soul*, 126.

163 New Life Clinics, *Simple Gifts: Unwrapping the Special Moments of Everyday Life* (Grand Rapids, Mich.: Zondervan, 1999).

164 Walsh, *Bring Back the Joy*, 52–53.

165 *Joy for a Woman's Soul*, 143.

166 Ibid., 32.

167 Ibid., 165.

168 Troccoli, 150–151.

169 *Joy for a Woman's Soul*, 145.

170 Ibid.

171 Walsh, *Living Fearlessly*, 38.

172 *Joy for a Woman's Soul*, 150.

173 New Life Clinics, *Simple Gifts*.

174 GRQ Ink, Inc., *Proverbs for Life for You* (Grand Rapids, Mich.: Zondervan, 2003), 73.

175 *Joy for a Woman's Soul*, 23.

176 Ibid., 89.

177 Ibid., 154.

178 Troccoli, 154–155.

179 *Women's Devotional Bible 2*, 693.

180 *Joy for a Woman's Soul*, 15.

181 Walsh, *Living Fearlessly*, 78.

182 Tada, *More Precious Than Silver*, September 7.

183 *Women's Devotional Bible 2*, 1300.

184 *Women's Devotional Bible 2*, 26.

185 Ibid., 62.

186 Ibid., 27.

187 Ibid., 151.

188 *Women's Devotional Bible 2*, 1309.

189 Troccoli, 159.

190 Women of Faith, Inc., *Bring Home the Joy* (Grand Rapids, Mich.: Zondervan, 1998), 20–21.

191 Walsh, *Living Fearlessly*, 80–81.

192 *Joy for a Woman's Soul*, 24.

193 Ibid., 30.

194 Tada, *More Precious Than Silver*, September 9.

195 New Life Clinics, *Laughter for a Woman's Soul*, 167.

196 *Joy for a Woman's Soul*, 33.

197 Tada, *Diamonds in the Dust*, April 10.

198 *Joy for a Woman's Soul*, 146.

199 Troccoli, 176–177.

200 Tada, *More Precious Than Silver*, September 13.

201 Walsh, *Living Fearlessly*, 87.

202 Tada, *Diamonds in the Dust*, April 25.

203 Clairmont, Johnson, Meberg, Swindoll, Walsh, Wells, *We Brake for Joy!* 259.

204 Tada, *Diamonds in the Dust*, September 25.

205 New Life Clinics, *Simple Gifts*.

206 *Women's Devotional Bible 2*, 552.

207 *Joy for a Woman's Soul*, 156.

208 Tada, *Diamonds in the Dust*, October 4.

209 Clairmont, Johnson, Meberg, Swindoll, Walsh, Wells, *We Brake for Joy!* 261–262.

210 Ibid., 42–43.

211 *Joy for a Woman's Soul*, 136.

212 Walsh, *Living Fearlessly*, 104.

213 *Joy for a Woman's Soul*, 59.

214 Tada, *Diamonds in the Dust*, October 13.

215 *Joy for a Woman's Soul*, 195.

216 Tada, *Diamonds in the Dust*, October 25.

217 *Joy for a Woman's Soul*, 36.

218 Troccoli, 187–188.

219 Tada, *Diamonds in the Dust*, December 5.

220 Clairmont, Johnson, Meberg, Swindoll, Walsh, Wells, *We Brake for Joy!* 263, 265.

221 *Joy for a Woman's Soul*, 133.

222 Walsh, *Living Fearlessly*, 146.

223 *Joy for a Woman's Soul*, 45.

224 Ibid., 198.

225 Ibid., 48.

226 *Women's Devotional Bible* (Grand Rapids, Mich.: Zondervan, 1990), 1175.

227 *Joy for a Woman's Soul*, 193.

228 Ibid., 38.

229 *Women's Devotional Bible*, 1368.

230 Troccoli, 180–181.

231 *Joy for a Woman's Soul*, 124.

232 Walsh, *Living Fearlessly*, 148–149.

233 *Joy for a Woman's Soul*, 39.

234 Ibid., 44.

235 Tada, *More Precious Than Silver*, January 19.

236 *Joy for a Woman's Soul*, 110.

237 Ibid., 192.

238 Tada, *More Precious Than Silver*, January 21.

239 *Joy for a Woman's Soul*, 42.

240 Tada, *More Precious Than Silver*, February 3.

241 *Joy for a Woman's Soul*, 109.

242 Ibid., 41.

243 Walsh, *Living Fearlessly*, 159.

244 Tada, *More Precious Than Silver*, February 5.

245 *Joy for a Woman's Soul*, 58.

246 Tada, *More Precious Than Silver*, February 12.

247 *Joy for a Woman's Soul*, 196.

248 Tada, *More Precious Than Silver*, February 5.

249 *Joy for a Woman's Soul*, 47.

250 Ibid., 115.

251 Ibid., 103.

252 Tada, *More Precious Than Silver*, February 17.

253 Walsh, *Living Fearlessly*, 170–171.

254 Tada, *More Precious Than Silver*, February 20.

255 *Joy for a Woman's Soul*, 172.

256 Ibid., 121.

257 Tada, *More Precious Than Silver*, February 20.

258 *Joy for a Woman's Soul*, 174.

259 Ibid., 139.

260 Tada, *More Precious Than Silver*, September 18.

261 *Joy for a Woman's Soul*, 100.

262 Tada, *More Precious Than Silver*, February 27.

263 Walsh, *Living Fearlessly*, 175–176.

264 Tada, *More Precious Than Silver*, March 5.

265 New Life Clinics, *Laughter for a Woman's Soul*, 160.

266 Tada, *More Precious Than Silver*, May 5.

267 *Joy for a Woman's Soul*, 137.

268 Tada, *More Precious Than Silver*, March 11.

269 *Joy for a Woman's Soul*, 181.

270 Tada, *More Precious Than Silver*, April 1.

271 *Joy for a Woman's Soul*, 88.

272 Walsh, *Living Fearlessly*, 177–178.

273 Tada, *More Precious Than Silver*, April 24.

274 Mullins, 33–34.

275 Tada, *More Precious Than Silver*, April 25.

276 *Joy for a Woman's Soul*, 189.

277 Tada, *More Precious Than Silver*, September 9.

278 *Joy for a Woman's Soul*, 127.

279 Tada, *More Precious Than Silver*, November 8.

280 *Joy for a Woman's Soul*, 86.

281 Tada, *More Precious Than Silver*, November 25.

282 Walsh, *Living Fearlessly*, 186.

283 Tada, *More Precious Than Silver*, September 13.

284 *Joy for a Woman's Soul*, 125.

285 Tada, *More Precious Than Silver*, November 28.

286 *Joy for a Woman's Soul*, 116.

287 Tada, *More Precious Than Silver*, December 13.

288 *Joy for a Woman's Soul*, 118.

289 Tada, *More Precious Than Silver*, September 22.

290 Clairmont, Johnson, Meberg, Swindoll, Walsh, Wells, *We Brake for Joy!* 40–41.

291 *Joy for a Woman's Soul*, 104.

292 Tada, *More Precious Than Silver*, December 16.

293 *Joy for a Woman's Soul*, 177.

294 George, *Tilling The Soul*, 115.

295 *Joy for a Woman's Soul*, 85.

296 Ibid., 113.

297 Walsh, *Honestly*, 164.

298 Tada, *More Precious Than Silver*, December 19.

299 *Joy for a Woman's Soul*, 101.

300 Clairmont, Johnson, Meberg, Swindoll, Walsh, Wells, *We Brake for Joy!* 15.

301 Ibid., 29.

302 Ibid., 25.

303 Tada, *More Precious Than Silver*, May 1.

304 *Joy for a Woman's Soul*, 190.

305 Tada, *More Precious Than Silver*, May 9.

306 John Wesley, *Spiritual Worship*, Sermon 77 (1781).

307 Tada, *More Precious Than Silver*, September 23.

308 Yancey, 205.

309 Clairmont, Johnson, Meberg, Swindoll, Walsh, Wells, *We Brake for Joy!* 19.

310 *Joy for a Woman's Soul*, 29.

311 Ibid., 159.

312 Clairmont, Johnson, Meberg, Swindoll, Walsh, Wells, *We Brake for Joy!* 75–76.

313 *Joy for a Woman's Soul*, 91.

At Inspirio we love to hear from you— your stories, your feedback, and your product ideas. Please send your comments to us by way of email at icares@zondervan.com or to the address below:

inspirio

Attn: Inspirio Cares
5300 Patterson Avenue SE
Grand Rapids, MI 49530

If you would like further information about Inspirio and the products we create, please visit us at: www.inspiriogifts.com

Thank you and God bless!